Readings: A New Biblical C

General Editor
John Jarick

FRANCIS CLOSE HAL'
LEARNI**

M A R K

MARK

Edwin K. Broadhead

www.SheffieldAcademicPress.com

Copyright © 2001 Sheffield Academic Press

Published by Sheffield Academic Press Ltd
Mansion House
19 Kingfield Road
Sheffield S11 9AS
England

www.SheffieldAcademicPress.com

Typeset by Sheffield Academic Press
and
Printed on acid-free paper in Great Britain
by Antony Rowe Ltd
Chippenham, Wiltshire

British Library Cataloguing in Publication Data

A catalogue record for this book is available
from the British Library

ISBN 1-84127-188-8 cloth
ISBN 1-84127-189-6 pb

To

Dempsey Matthew Broadhead

source of encouragement

Contents

Preface

I am grateful for the invitation from Sheffield Academic Press to contribute to the *Readings* commentary series. This invitation provides an unusual opportunity to bring together some ten years of research into the Gospel of Mark into a format accessible to a wider audience. My journey with the Gospel of Mark began in a Greek reading class under Alan Culpepper. This was followed by a year of study under Ulrich Luz at the University of Bern, Switzerland. Under his guidance and that of my colleague Peter Lampe, I worked through the major German commentaries on the Gospel of Mark—in particular those of Rudolph Pesch and Joachim Gnilka. Following this year of research I began an intensive study of the miracle stories in the Gospel of Mark. At the same time that I was pursuing this critical research I found practical application by preaching through the Gospel of Mark at Jordan Baptist Church in Eagle Station, Kentucky. My research on the miracles was accepted as a doctoral dissertation and subsequently published through Sheffield's JSOT Press as *Teaching with Authority: Miracles and Christology in the Gospel of Mark*. This was followed by doctoral studies at the University of Zürich under the guidance of Hans Weder and Eduard Schweizer. My Zürich dissertation was published by Sheffield as *Prophet, Son, Messiah: Narrative Form and Function in Mark 14-16*. A third volume on the role of the titles was published by Sheffield Academic Press as *Naming Jesus: Titular Christology in the Gospel of Mark*. I am grateful for the opportunity to bring together these works, as well as numerous other critical articles, to provide a narrative commentary on the entirety of this Gospel.

I am grateful for those who have helped me on my way. A particular debt is owed to colleagues from within the Society of Biblical Literature and from the Society for New Testament Studies for ongoing dialogue and friendships from which such works grow. I am also grateful to Berea College for their support and encouragement to find time for such projects. Many of the ideas presented here were first tested on a weekly faculty Bible study, where I was required to articulate critical concepts in palatable language. I am especially glad for the many conversations shared with my wife and colleague, Loretta Reynolds, who brings to this text vital questions from her own field of homiletics.

This text is dedicated to Dempsey Matthew Broadhead, my father. I have learned from him countless lessons of life and faith and love and endurance. I have received from him an overabundance of listening and patience and encouragement. Among his many gifts to me is the love of critical scholarship. When I gathered his professional contributions into a volume which was presented to him, his published works exceeded 75. With much love and pride, I am pleased to dedicate this volume to him.

Edwin K. Broadhead
Ash Wednesday, 2000

Abbreviations

BJRL	*Bulletin of the John Rylands University Library of Manchester*
CGTC	Cambridge Greek Testament Commentary
EKKNT	Evangelisch-Katholischer Kommentar zum Neuen Testament
EvT	*Evangelische Theologie*
HTKNT	Herders theologischer Kommentar zum Neuen Testament
JBL	*Journal of Biblical Literature*
JR	*Journal of Religion*
JSNTSup	*Journal for the Study of the New Testament*, Supplement Series
JTS	*Journal of Theological Studies*
MIT	Massachusetts Institute of Technology
MNTC	Moffatt NT Commentary
NCB	New Century Bible
NICNT	New International Commentary on the New Testament
OTNT	Ökumenischer Taschenbuchkommentar zum Neuen Testament
RevExp	*Review and Expositor*
SANT	Studien zum Alten und Neuen Testament
SBB	Stuttgarter biblische Beiträge
SBLDS	SBL Dissertation Series
THKNT	Theologischer Handkommentar zum Neuen Testament
WBC	Word Biblical Commentary
ZNW	*Zeitschrift für die neutestamentliche Wissenschaft*
ZTK	*Zeitschrift für Theologie und Kirche*

Introduction

When ancient cartographers reached the limits of their knowledge they wrote a note across uncharted regions of the map: 'Here be dragons.' This warning prevented most sailors from venturing past the limits. Others took this notice not as a warning, but as an invitation and sailed boldly into uncharted waters. They discovered there new worlds, and they rewrote the maps of antiquity.

Thus the reader stands at the beginning of this Gospel, for there are mysteries here yet unfathomed. With the opening line—'The beginning of the Gospel of Jesus Christ...'—the reader is issued a warning and an invitation: here are uncharted waters, new worlds, untold stories.

'Let the reader understand!'—this warning from Mk 13.14 is timely not only for the first reader, but for all who read this story. Recent research in Gospel studies has rediscovered the literary dimensions of this text, and renewed attention has been given to the process of reading and to its effect upon the reader. As a result a host of strategies may be seen at work in this Gospel, drawing readers into a complex web of questions and claims about the story of Jesus. This commentary offers a reading of the Gospel of Mark; this reading is informed by the insights of narrative criticism and seeks to unveil for the reader the strategies at work in these stories. While the approach of such a commentary is necessarily analytical, the goal is more holistic: to open this ancient text to modern reading and to invite contemporary readers to negotiate the claims of this story for their own context.

No text nor reader is wholly innocent and without bias. Readers bring to texts their own experiences, presumptions and agendas. Texts offer a biased view of the world and may prove insistent in their claims. Texts can mislead readers and readers can misread texts. The negotiation of meaning, like the dance of the cobra and the mongoose, is sometimes a dangerous task. One line of study in narratives—formalism, structuralism and narratology—insists the first task is to identify how the text is constructed. Attention is given not only to the parts that make up the story, but also to the arrangement of these elements. Uses of setting, plot, characterization, narration are identified. Particular patterns of language, symbolism, literary devices are observed. This approach takes seriously the strategy of the text at hand as it offers its story to readers. A second line gives attention more to the consumer of the text. Reader-response theories ask who is reading this text, what are their presumptions and biases, what are their expectations and competencies, what effect does the text create. To some degree the text is judged by its impact on the reader. A text that does not address the need of the reader—for justice or liberation, for example—may be judged to be irrelevant at best and oppressive at worst. These two lines of approach are not necessarily exclusive. Few scholars now believe that a text, even a biblical text, can speak one message with one voice for all times and places and people. Few critics think that all readings of a text are equal and that meaning lies wholly in what readers think they read. The most productive realm of interpretation is found in the interplay between what the text offers to the reader and what the reader brings to the text.

As a consequence several elements are imperative for a narrative commentary on the Gospel of Mark. The first of these is a clear analysis, stated in palatable language, of what goes on in the text. What is the story told? Where is it told, when is it told and who is telling it? What narrative components are used and how are these arranged? What characters inhabit the story and how are they developed? What information is conveyed? What claims are made? The second requirement for a narrative commentary is some awareness of who is reading the text and what is happening in the process of reading.

In recent years the literary dimensions of the Gospels have been reclaimed, and these are now placed alongside historical and textual developments as key elements for interpretation. Thus a commentary that focuses on the process of reading can be one component in the larger task of understanding and appropriating the message of a Gospel. This process may be compared to a musical event. The Gospel of Mark offers a score—a script with a long and complex history of composition and transmission. Close analysis brings to light the complexity of its development and arrangement. But the script cannot perform itself, and no amount of analysis can bring the score to life. Ultimately good stories, like good music, live through performance. Each performance of a play or a symphony or a Gospel is unique, but those that embody and interpret and enhance the script or the score or the text are most valued. Like good music and good theatre, good reading is an event; it is guided by the script, but performed by the reader. This commentary seeks to facilitate such a reading of the Gospel of Mark.

A Sacred Text

The Gospel of Mark is a sacred text. It is sacred not only because of its internal claims, but also because it is held to be sacred by many of its readers. This text claims to present a sacred message that places distinct religious demands upon its readers. Those who recorded these stories and transmitted them through the Christian tradition held this text to be sacred. Thus the sacred claim becomes an inherent characteristic of this literature. Some readers, modern and ancient, choose to reject this claim. This is the prerogative of all who read; indeed, it is the responsibility of every reader to negotiate the degree to which the sacred dimensions of a text are relevant for the reader. The rejection of the sacred claims of a text does not, however, remove those claims. Whether or not a reader is receptive, the sacred claims remain an intrinsic part of this literature. To study the Gospel of Mark as anything other than sacred is to redefine its genre and to create an alternate form of literature.

At the same time the Gospel of Mark is literature. It was composed under the influence of literary traditions, and it has been transmitted through the channels of literary development, including a complicated textual history. This Gospel has a plot, a narrator, a set of characters, a temporal and geographical setting. A wide range of genres are employed in the telling of this tale. It makes use of symbolism, allegory, alliteration, chiasm, word plays, intercalations, frames, triads and a host of other literary devices. The Gospel of Mark is, in the evaluation of many literary critics, a tale well told.

An authentic reading of this Gospel must hold both dimensions—the sacred and the literary—in constant tension. The sacred claims of the text do not exempt it from analysis as a piece of literature constructed and transmitted within a historical framework. Analysis of the literary dimensions of this Gospel do not extinguish its sacred history or its sacred potential. This reading of the Gospel of Mark presumes throughout that this text expresses sacred claim precisely through its literary dimensions.

An Engaged Reader

This analysis of the Gospel of Mark also presumes an engaged reader. The literary dimensions of the text cannot be comprehended by computer analysis, and a hostile reading of the text—an anti-reading—lies outside the interest of this study. At a minimum the reader is assumed to be competent in the language in which they read, the reader is presumed to be able to pick up basic literary cues and the reader is presumed to care. This does not mean the reader affirms the message of the text, but it does mean the reader has competence and interest to support the performance of the text.

A Strategy for Reading

Since there are many strategies for reading and many points of beginning for readers, it is important to clarify the stance and strategy behind this reading of the Gospel of Mark.

The Situation of the Text

While the situation of the Gospel of Mark is debated among New Testament scholars, this commentary will proceed from a clear set of presumptions about the historical setting. The text that we read as the Gospel of Mark comes into present form somewhere around the time of the second Jewish War, that is the late 60s or early 70s of the first century. Mark 13 suggests the composition of the Gospel is closely connected to the fall of the temple in 70 CE. Within the story the ethos is Jewish, but the outlook of the story is strongly Galilean. There is unusual diffidence, if not disdain, for the organized cultic piety of Judaism and there is extended controversy with Jewish religious leaders. Jerusalem plays no positive role in the story, serving only as the hostile city in which Jesus, upon his one visit there, meets his death. The majority of scenes are set in an itinerant mission among the peasant villages of Galilee and surrounding Gentile regions. The story has strong connections to the movement of John the Baptist. Thus the story is told at the margins of Judaism.

While Christian tradition has designated Mark as the author of the text and has identified this figure with John Mark from Jerusalem, this designation has little historical support. From a literary standpoint the idea of a single author who composes the Gospel within a short time frame is unlikely. A more probable scenario is that the Gospel of Mark represents a large body of community tradition that was collected, written in common Greek and used within a Galilean community. This text served as the foundational document by which this community lived. Conversely, the experience of this community in worship, missions and self-identification shaped the formation of the text over a number of years. While the text drew upon the story of Jesus, now some 40 years past, the primary concern was provided by the questions and crises faced by this marginal community in the late 60s and early 70s. This community draws upon memories of Jesus as a historical figure, but its story is told selectively in order to address the current needs of this community. As such the text represents an alternate form of Judaism centred on the following of Jesus and consciously concerned for the place of the Gentiles. This story, told at the margins of Jewish life amid the instability of the 70s, exhibits a strong interest in the overcoming of boundaries—

social, physical, religious, geographical—and this too reflects the situation of the community.

The Situation of the Reader

While contemporary readers may inform themselves about the historical,
religious and social setting of this Gospel, it is impossible to read as a
first-century reader. Great differences in world-view, competencies, presumptions and expectations intervene between the world of the first
century and the reader of the twenty-first century. Likewise not all readers of the twenty-first century share the same competence or presumptions. Each reader and each reading is bound by the particularities of
who they are and where they are, by what they presume and by what
they expect. This commentary is based on the reading of a middle-class
male of European descent with competence in both the Greek text and
the conventions of contemporary literary criticism. This reader has a
strong association with the rural and agrarian setting of the Gospel, with
its patterns of resistance to traditional structures and with its transna-
tional perspective.

Questions Raised by the Text

The Gospel of Mark is not an even-handed historical report. Specific
events from this era are highlighted at the expense of others. Even
within the story of Jesus, the reporting is selective. For example, the last
week of Jesus' life is given three chapters (14–16), but nothing is said of
his early life. Those episodes that are selected are narrated within carefully arranged frameworks. Distinct characterizations are created, resulting in heroes and villains and ficelles. This Gospel has an agenda, and the
first item on the list is Christology—the question of who Jesus is. The
opening lines set the pattern, the question is placed on the lips of disciples and observers and the story line is never far from the question 'Who
do you say that I am?' (Mk 8.29). Through titles, parables, miracles, controversy and discourse the Gospel consistently poses the question of the
identity of Jesus.

The second major concern is found in the issue of discipleship. The
framing of Jesus' identity is the catalyst for the call to follow him. A variety of demands are posed, and a host of responses are narrated. From
the actions of religious leaders, crowds, the Twelve, those with him, the
reader is offered a range of responses to Jesus and his call.

A third concern is the controversy that follows the story of Jesus. This
conflict is sometimes initiated by Jesus, sometimes by others. His ministry is accompanied by rejection and hostility, by widespread misunderstanding and finally by the death plot. Prior to the story of Jesus, John

the Baptist dies for his message. A similar fate is foreseen for disciples who come after Jesus. Controversy frames and inhabits all of the story of Jesus.

These major concerns are brought under a single focus in the opening chapter. The message from God which Jesus announces and enacts is this: the Reign of God is near. Jesus' words and deeds, the call to discipleship and the conflict which this engenders are all components of the call to the Kingdom. What is the nature and reality of the Kingdom? Who is Jesus, and what does it mean to follow him? Do conflict and defeat and death signal the failure of Jesus and the end of this movement, or is there more? These are the questions that the Gospel of Mark places before its readers.

Questions Raised by the Reader

The questions raised by the first-century reader emerge at points in the story. How do we keep the Jewish sabbath (Mk 2.23-28)? Shall we fast (Mk 2.18-22)? Shall we keep the tradition of the elders (Mk 7.1-13)? What should we eat (Mk 7.14-23)? How do we relate to Gentiles, to women and children (Mk 7.24-30)? How does the war in Jerusalem relate to the end of the world (Mk 13)? What is the significance of Jesus' execution? These and other questions show the intent of the community to relate the story of Jesus to their own situation.

The reader of the twenty-first century brings a different set of questions to the story. Issues such as the fate of Jerusalem and the maintenance of Jewish identity are distant concerns. They are replaced by different interests. Among the questions underlying this commentary are the following. Can the story of Jesus have relevance for contemporary life? Who is Jesus for today, and what does it mean to follow him? Is discipleship best lived in institutional contexts, or do these deter obedience? Does the Gospel offer a way to cross modern boundaries between humans? Does the Gospel of Mark contain a vision of humanity and an agenda for justice which is applicable in modern life? Can the concept of the Kingdom of God provide a program for reconciliation between humans and God, between humans and other humans, between humans and the environment?

Levels of Analysis

This strategy for reading the Gospel of Mark will operate along four levels of analysis. The first level is that of morphology—what the text contains. Is the story one continuous event, or is it composed of episodes? What genres are employed? Are these used in traditional form, or have they been reshaped in the telling of the story? What patterns of structuring are used? What are the components of the individual stories and of the larger story?

The second level of analysis is that of syntax—how the components of the story are arranged, what relationship they have to each other. Attention will be given to dynamics such as order, style, symbolism, structure, interplay, intertextual connections, intratextual references, allusions.

The third level of analysis is that of signification. When the components of the text are presented through various literary patterns, what does this signify within the world of the text? What is the world-view created here? What does the text claim about Jesus, about other characters, about its own message? What is not said here? Such narrative significance is not a subjective value dependent upon the mood of the reader. The formal components and dynamics of the text create a literary sign that is measurable in the same way that the sense of a sentence is measurable. Just as the proper syntactical combination of a subject and verb and modifiers can create a linguistic sign with clear significance ('all children hate spinach'), so significance may be created at the narrative level through the syntactical arrangement of literary elements. Not all will agree that the significance is true or that it is relevant (some children like spinach), but the point and claim of the sentence is clear. So with the Gospel of Mark. For example, Mk 4.35-41 uses a traditional form of miracle story to signify that Jesus has distinct power to command nature to silence, then places this claim in contrast to the fear and cowardice of his followers. Whether the reader accepts or rejects this claim is beside the point, at least for now. What the narrative claims is clear. Numerous components and various dynamics combine to create the narrative sign or claim that Jesus is an unusual miracle worker. A key component in this commentary is narrative significance—what signs and realities and claims are created by the narrative.

The fourth level of analysis is that of meaning. Meaning is found in what the reader does with the text. A closed text has significance in that it has a story to tell, but a closed text has no meaning. What the text means emerges in the dance and negotiation that occurs in the reading process. Readings may be evaluated as good or bad by how well they reflect the components and dynamics and signs of the text; thus, not all readings are equal. At the same time, no text can wholly determine its own meaning. Some readers reject the claims of the text; some accept them; some are indifferent. To return to the example from Mark 4, the claim that Jesus is a powerful miracle worker is clear. What is not yet clear is whether that claim has historical credibility and, more importantly, whether that claim has any continuing relevance in a scientific age. If this claim means anything, what it means must emerge from the hermeneutical struggle to find the meaning of the text in the world of the reader.

Patterns of the Commentary

What follows is a narrative commentary that seeks to guide the reading of this Gospel. While a strong concern for the historical situation of this Gospel and for issues of methodology underlies this analysis, the reader is directed to the bibliography for discussion of these issues. The outline of the Gospel of Mark used in this commentary is not the traditional one. Narrative analysis will show that many stories overlap in this Gospel. Numerous verses which serve the purpose of transition properly belong to both of the stories they serve. The structural outline used in this commentary seeks to reflect these narrative traits of overlap and interconnection. A literary analysis will be applied to sequential episodes of the story. A developing plot line and emerging lines of characterization will be identified. Larger sections of material will be defined along structural and thematic lines, and the role of individual episodes within these sections will be considered. This analysis will conclude with examination from the perspective of the entire Gospel. While historical issues and methodological concerns are never far from the surface of the discussion, the primary goal here is to enact a strategy for reading the Gospel of Mark and to examine the impact and the potential of this performance.

Mark 1.1-20: The Gospel Begins

The opening sections of the Gospel of Mark spell out the major themes to be developed through the flow of the story. This strategy creates a primacy effect, lending extraordinary focus to the opening scenes. This strategy also unveils the pattern of the story: the concerns introduced here will be revisited and developed throughout the plot line. Like the overture of a symphony, Mk 1.1-20 presents the themes that will be reprised and completed through the flow of the story. An architectural motif is also appropriate: the first act of building is to stake out the construction site, and this section sets the parameters for the scenes that follow.

Staking out the Story (Mark 1.1-8)

The Gospel of Mark opens with the voice of the narrator explaining the nature of the story which is about to unfold (Mk 1.1-3). In literary perspective the narrator is a persona within the text who guides the reader through the story. The narrator may be a reliable or unreliable figure, and this figure may or may not share the author's positions. In the Gospel of Mark the narrator is reliable and seems to represent the voice of the implied author of the text.

In this story the narrator intrudes infrequently to provide information or to guide the reading of the story. In the Gospel of Mark showing almost always takes priority over telling; this is a gospel of events and deeds rather than one of words and reports. This means that the opening comments from the narrator are unusual, and such a lengthy intrusion will not be repeated.

The narrator's opening first tells what the story is, yet even this is unclear. What is begun here is the gospel of Jesus Christ, but does this mean that verse 1 is the beginning and that the entire story is the Gospel? Or does this mean that the entire story tells of the beginning of the gospel of Jesus? The former seems more probable, since the next verses point to the beginning of Jesus' ministry. Also unclear is whether the gospel is the message that Jesus proclaims or the message proclaimed about Jesus. This is an important distinction: the message proclaimed by Jesus was the nearness of the Kingdom of God, while the message proclaimed about Jesus is that he is God's son, the messiah. While both elements are present in the Gospel of Mark, the story of what Jesus proclaimed serves as the catalyst and guide for what is to be proclaimed about Jesus.

In telling how the Gospel begins, the narrator also tells of who Jesus is. He is named in the opening line as the Christ (or messiah) and, in many ancient manuscripts, as the son of God. This seems proper, but the reader will soon discover that the rest of the story is hesitant to give such titles to Jesus.

A third piece of information is given through the citation in 1.2-3: the story of Jesus stands in continuity with the prophetic promises of the Old Testament. Such direct intertextual connections are unusual in the Gospel of Mark, and they almost always occur on the lips of Jesus. Here Scripture is quoted by the narrator in order to connect the story of John (Mk 1.4-8) to the Old Testament promise. Furthermore, the citation is credited (incorrectly) to the prophet Isaiah. Mark 1.2 is drawn from Mal. 3.1 and Mk 1.3 is drawn from Isaiah 40.

Thus, the Gospel of Mark begins in a rather awkward and unexpected way. A voice that is external to the plot line of the story tells the reader what the narrative is about, who Jesus is and how this connects to the Old Testament. The only similar narration is found at the end of the story (16.1-8), where an unusual messenger tells the women at the tomb that Jesus has been raised and will go before them into Galilee. Despite the awkward nature of this entrance, the information provided at the beginning of the story provides an important context for the reader: whatever events occur in this narrative are a part of the good news of Jesus, who is the messiah and the son of God. Furthermore, the appearance of John is shown to be a preparing of the way for God's new work.

In the story of John the Baptist (1.4-8) the narrative finds its normal voice. Telling gives way to showing, and the voice of the narrator is disguised by the events of the story. The emphasis on the nature of the gospel and the character of Jesus continues, but in a different mode of presentation. The short, condensed, action-oriented style which typifies this Gospel is heard in the opening scene: clothed in the garb of a prophet, John appears in the wilderness preaching repentance, and the people come from everywhere to be baptized by him. In three brief sentences the life of a complex, intriguing figure is presented to the reader. Apart from the later story of John's death (6.14-29) and a few passing references (1.14; 8.28), the story of John unfolds in these few phrases.

Having established the voice of John, his role in the story is accomplished in 1.7-8. There he announces that a coming figure will surpass his own ministry and that this messenger will baptize in the Holy Spirit. These few short strokes set the stage for the appearance of Jesus. The story is identified as good news connected with his name. The backdrop for the larger story is found in the claim that Jesus is the messiah and the son of God. John is shown as the prophetic messenger who prepares the way for God's new work, and the expectation is set for one who will come in the power of God's Spirit. The theological significance of these historical characters and events is articulated precisely through this literary strategy of presentation.

Staking out the Identity of Jesus (Mark 1.9-13)

While the opening line offers a rare telling of who Jesus is, the more typical pattern of showing is found in Mk 1.9-13. The information that 'Jesus came from Nazareth of Galilee' brings him in proximity to John, but this phrase also offers a summary of his prior life. Moving forward from his identification with Nazareth, Jesus is identified with the movement and baptism of John. Unlike in other Gospels, no explanation or disclaimer qualifies Jesus' submission to John's call to be baptized. This identification can be observed by others in the story and is made plain to the reader.

The next stage of identification is seemingly not available to bystanders, but only to Jesus and the reader. In other scenes onlookers respond to miracles with acclamation and wonder, but the voice of the crowd is missing here. When he comes up from the baptismal waters Jesus sees the heavens opened and observes the Spirit descending upon him (1.10). The identity of Jesus is confirmed for the reader in the voice which Jesus hears: this is the beloved son of God.

One further layer of identification is added to Jesus' portrait, and this too is a private experience available only to Jesus and to the reader of the story. Showing and telling are combined in a terse account. Jesus' sojourn in the wilderness is instigated by the Spirit, who drives him out (1.12). His days in the wilderness are marked by the presence of the tempter, by the companionship of wild beasts and by the ministry of angels. Here the story enters a world that is unfamiliar to the modern reader. Historical analysis cannot document the presence of angelic or demonic figures, and few creatures survive in the Judaean desert. The reader has been asked to step into another world—one drawn from Old Testament images of exodus and exile. Like Israel, Jesus finds in the wilderness sojourn both conflict and consolation, and it is here that he, like Israel, comes to the fullness of his identity.

Through these images and moves the Gospel offers a glimpse into the private identity of Jesus. Emerging from the movement of John, Jesus bears the marks of Israel's history. Endorsed by the ancient voice of Yahweh and driven by God's Spirit, Jesus steps onto the stage of history and into the flow of the story.

Staking out the Ministry and Message of Jesus (Mark 1.14-20)

The story turns from who Jesus is to what he does, and telling gives way wholly to showing. The ministry and message of Jesus are identified in two brief movements: he comes into Galilee and he walks beside the lake. The context of Jesus' ministry is found in John's imprisonment. Both temporal and ideological connections are suggested. 'After John's imprisonment' tells not only the timing of Jesus' activity: the crisis of John's arrest and imminent death initiates Jesus' ministry and sets its tone.

The place of Jesus' activity is clarified. From the wilderness he comes into the Galilee, and there his story unfolds. The task is made clear: preaching good news from God, about God. The message is articulated: the time is full, the Kingdom of God is near. The demand is set forth: repent and believe in the gospel. Thus, the heart of Jesus' ministry is unveiled in his first activity and his first words.

The final component of Jesus' ministry is found in the call scene of 1.16-20. The scene occurs as a doublet, first with Simon and Andrew, then with James and John. Three elements comprise these simple scenes: Jesus issues a direct and unqualified call—come, follow me; the fishers leave something behind; they go after Jesus.

Summary

The Gospel of Mark accomplishes a great deal of work in its opening scenes. As a result the reader has heard the major chords of the story and is familiar with its parameters. Through a minimal amount of telling the reader has been introduced to the central characters and themes of this Gospel. Perhaps just as significant is what the reader is not told. No account is given of pre-human origins, the story of Jesus' birth and childhood is bypassed and internal motivations are not observed. The gospel story begins with the work of John and unfolds the hope of the prophets. Jesus of Nazareth, a member of John's movement, is anointed by the Spirit, endorsed by the voice of God and tested by wilderness sojourn. His own activity begins with the announcement that God has come to reign and the demand for repentance and faith. His work is accompanied by common workers who heed his call. Upon this stage the story of the gospel will unfold.

Mark 1.21-3.7a: The Authority of Jesus

In the opening act of this Gospel Jesus makes his residence in Capernaum, then ministers in the surrounding villages and beside the lake.
The authority of Jesus is demonstrated in the wonders he performs, in
his call to disciples and in his conflict with religious leaders. Through
these scenes key elements are added to the characterization of Jesus and
new dimensions are given to his work.

On the First Day:
The Great Sabbath in Capernaum (Mark 1.21-39)

This unit is composed of three scenes, each of which uses a distinct literary form. The initial scene (1.23-28) is an exorcism story. The first
reader might recognize that the story follows a fixed form and contains
elements found in miracle accounts from Jewish storytellers or Hellenis-
tic writers. This exorcism scene has a clear introduction (1.23-24) and a
body in which the action occurs (1.25-26) and is followed by reflection
upon the event (1.27-28). The conclusion of the scene involves physical
movement to another place (1.29). Various elements within the scene
are typical of the way miracles are narrated. The miracle worker moves
onto the scene. A problem and a victim are introduced, and the difficulty
of the crisis is demonstrated. The miracle worker responds to the challenge. A dramatic scene accompanies the healing. Wonder and acclamation are expressed by those who observe the healing. The report of the
event spreads far beyond the observers.

The second scene is an abbreviated healing story (1.29-31). This story
also employs a familiar pattern: the healer moves into the scene, the
victim is introduced and the difficulty of the disease is discussed, the
healing is accomplished through some physical act, then demonstration
of the healing is provided.

The third scene is a summary that encapsulates numerous healings
(1.32-38). This scene is framed by the movement of the people to Jesus
at the end of the sabbath period (1.32-33) and by Jesus' departure at the
end of the scene (1.35-38). The heart of the story is found in 1.34, which
summarizes various types of healing given to a host of victims. The
command to silence given to the demons is also a typical element from
such stories.

Thus, the episode in Mk 1.21-39 is composed of three scenes told in story patterns familiar to the first reader. Though typical story forms are used, how these stories are told is also important. Various elements within the scenes lend colour and link them uniquely to the ministry of Jesus. In the exorcism story (1.23-28) the plot action centres around the possessed man, but this plot development is linked to the characterization of Jesus. Within the story this is accomplished by the questions of the people: 'What is this—a new teaching with authority? He commands even the unclean spirits and they obey him' (1.27). In addition, the report about Jesus circulates throughout the Galilee (1.28). The key identification of Jesus occurs in the cry of the victim. Having been anointed by the Spirit of God (1.10), Jesus is recognized by the powers of the spirit world. 'What to you and to me?' they cry out, describing Jesus as 'the Nazarene' and as 'the Holy One of God'. Jesus' reply echoes the rough speech of the demons and leads to their violent departure. Thus, the formal exorcism pattern has been stretched into a character portrait of Jesus: he is the Holy One who enters into the realm of the spirits and casts them out, and the report of his deeds is spreading.

The new element in the healing scene (1.29-31) is the presence of the four fishers called to follow Jesus. The presence of these first disciples at the scene of the healing is not developed within the story, but it adds a new dimension to their characterization. The response of the healed woman is a typical element that validates the healing, but here she serves them. This element will also prove significant in the developing profile of discipleship.

The summary scene also establishes a key literary motif. The silencing of demons is a typical element, but the potential of this command will be developed later in the narrative. Thus, standard literary forms have been used to show the nature of Jesus' ministry. Various elements within the stories guide these scenes toward the function of characterization. In particular, these scenes add further dimensions to the character sketch of Jesus, and they pose the issue of what it means to follow him.

In addition to these internal characteristics, the linkage of the three scenes creates a new literary context. This is accomplished primarily through the movement that frames this episode. In 1.21 Jesus and his group enter into Capernaum, and they enter into the Jewish synagogue. At the end of the episode Jesus declares his intention to 'go elsewhere' (1.38), then travels throughout the Galilee.

Another type of frame is created around the temporal markers in this episode. The story opens on the sabbath (1.21), which is the setting for the first two scenes. The healing summary (1.32-34) occurs with the setting of the sun, which marks the end of the sabbath (1.32). The episode concludes with their departure early the next morning (1.35). Thus, the entire episode is set as a single day within the ministry of Jesus. From a literary perspective this is the first day of Jesus' ministry, and it is a sabbath day.

The unity of the three scenes may also be seen in their structure. The first scene does not have a developed conclusion. At the end of the story Jesus goes from the synagogue and enters the house of Peter and Andrew. This ending serves also as the beginning of the second scene. The second scene has no conclusion, but leads abruptly into the third. This tailoring of beginnings and endings creates a smooth transition from one scene to the next and encourages the reader to see here a single episode.

The most important frame for these scenes is found in the transition to and from the episode. The opening lines define the activity of Jesus in Capernaum as teaching (1.21). The following lines describe the amazement of the hearers, then sets the teaching of Jesus over against that of the scribes (1.22). In this way the reader is encouraged to see the activity in the synagogue as an example of Jesus' teaching and the authority it carries. The normal expectation for a reader, in the first century or the twenty-first, is to see Jesus' teaching demonstrated in what he says and in how he says it. The Gospel of Luke follows this expectation by linking this scene to Jesus' words and to his fulfilment of the Old Testament writings (Lk. 4.14-44). The Gospel of Matthew associates the power of Jesus' teaching with the carefully crafted words of the Sermon on the Mount (Mt. 7.28-29). What is expected in light of Mk 1.21-22 is the ministry of the word; what is given is not word, but extraordinary deeds. The Gospel of Mark asks the reader to understand Jesus' wondrous deeds as indicative of his power as a teacher sent from God.

A similar association is created at the end of the episode. When he learns that the crowds are seeking him out, Jesus insists that he must go to the surrounding villages. 'There also I will preach', Jesus says, 'for this reason I came out' (1.38). Through these lines the activity at Capernaum is (re)defined in retrospect as a preaching ministry. This means that preaching and teaching are synonyms within the Gospel of Mark and that the wondrous deeds of Jesus demonstrate the authority of his teaching/preaching.

In this way the events at Capernaum are framed as a single sabbath day that inaugurates the ministry of Jesus. The dramatic events that occur here and their unusual connection to the authority of Jesus as teacher set the pattern for Jesus' ministry and bring stark new dimensions to his profile. The impact of this episode is not localized, however, for the closing lines indicate that he will repeat these scenes in synagogues and villages throughout the Galilee (1.38-39).

Within the larger episode, significant lines are crossed. Jesus enters into the realm of the spirits and releases one who is bound by their power. While this world-view may seem strange to the modern reader, it is a coherent realm of the first reader's world-view. A fixed boundary has been crossed, and a human victim has been released. The release of the woman from the fever echoes these images of liberation.

The boundary between clean and unclean is also crossed when the man is released from the demons. This boundary has medical and psychological and religious dimensions and provides a key point of reference within the first reader's world. Later events in the narrative will develop this motif further.

Another set of boundaries is crossed in the development of this episode. The scene begins within the typical Jewish religious setting of the synagogue. Jesus' power is here contrasted to that of the scribes who record and transmit the teachings of Judaism. The next scene locates the power of Jesus within the house, and this setting will become an important element of the Gospel. The summary scene occurs outside in the village, and this too will undergo development. The final lines insist that these scenes will be replicated throughout the synagogues and villages of the Galilee. In this way the religious authority of Jesus moves outward from the traditional setting of Jewish worship into the streets and homes and villages of the people.

The focus on the preaching and teaching of Jesus links this episode to the larger story. The first mention of Jesus' proclamation notes that he preaches the nearness of God's Reign (1.15). For the attentive reader the connection lies close at hand: here in the dramatic deeds of Jesus' preaching—typified on a sabbath at Capernaum but realized on various days throughout Galilee—the Kingdom of God is drawing near.

The characterization of Jesus has taken on new dimensions. He who was announced as messiah and son of God by the narrator (1.1) and as the beloved son by the voice from heaven (1.11) has been declared by demons as the Holy One from God (1.24). The authority of his teaching is demonstrated in his deeds of wonder and stands in stark contrast to that of the scribes.

A profile for discipleship is also underway. Called from their labours on the lake (1.16-20), the disciples witness the scenes in Capernaum and accompany Jesus on his journey through the villages of the Galilee.

The primacy effect of this three-part episode is crucial. Established on the first day as the pattern for all of Jesus' days, the wondrous teaching of Jesus is reported (1.28) and practiced (1.39) throughout the region. Like ripples on a calm lake, these images will flow through the entirety of the Gospel story.

Healing a Leper; Confronting Israel (Mark 1.39-45)

This episode also employs a standard story form to tell of the healing of a leper. The victim takes the initiative and introduces himself into the story. The difficulty of the disease is evident when he is named as a leper—some rabbis thought the healing of a leper to be more difficult than the raising of the dead. The authority of the healer is acknowledged, and the healing is accomplished through a touch. The victim is dismissed, and the response of the crowd is mentioned.

Various elements within this standard form are noteworthy. The story speaks throughout not of healing, but of a cleansing. Within the medical terminology of the era this is appropriate, but it also speaks of the religious and social dimensions of leprosy. As articulated in the Levitical code (Lev. 14-15), the leper is separated from the sacred realms of Jewish life and from the patterns of daily social discourse. The leper has been declared unclean, and only a declaration by the priest can restore religious and social status.

Also worthy of note is the faith of the leper in Jesus' ability. Because the victim is a leper who is untouchable, the healing touch is poignant. It not only provides the healing act, but it also signals the restoration of the victim to human status. A significant twist is found in the dismissal of the healed victim. In language that is harsh and reflects the exorcism stories ('he cast him out'), the healed leper is dismissed and is commanded to tell no one what has happened.

The most significant development is found in the command for the victim to go to the priest. The victim is to take the offering commanded by Moses for the healing of leprosy, and this act will serve as a witness (1.44). Does Jesus wish to fulfil the details of the Levitical code and to gain the approval of the priest? This seems strange in a story where Jesus resists cultic dimensions of worship and engages in ongoing controversy with the religious leaders of Israel. The language of this phrase clearly demands a witness before the priest; what the language does not specify is the nature of this witness. The linguistic construction may imply 'as a witness to them', but this phrase is used often in the Gospels, in the New Testament and in other Greek writings to mean 'against them'. That is how the witness should be read in this story. In the Levitical code it was the priest who declared a leper unclean, and it was a priest who had the power to declare the leper clean. In this story it is Jesus who has declared the leper clean. When the leper stands before the priest, a living testimony is given: you have declared me unclean, but you were not able to make me clean. In contrast to this impotence stands the power of Jesus, who has restored the victim to normal human status. The form of the story is thus stretched to accommodate another story pattern—the controversy scene. This tension between Jesus and the religious leadership of Israel will echo throughout this Gospel, and Jesus is, on occasion, the instigator of the conflict. The opening lines of this debate are sounded precisely in the story of the leper. The teaching authority of Jesus is displayed in his wonders, and his power stands in stark contrast to that of the scribes (1.22) and to that of the priests of Israel (1.44).

In addition to using a standard form with various literary twists, this story is shaped by the framework in which it is placed. The opening transition in 1.39 connects the scene to the previous stories, but particularly to the emerging pattern of Jesus' ministry. What Jesus did in Capernaum he does throughout the Galilee: he preaches in their synagogues and he casts out demons. From 1.14-15 the reader knows that what Jesus preaches is the Kingdom of God; from the Capernaum story the reader knows that the miracles demonstrate the authority of Jesus' teaching. The healing of the leper belongs to this larger itinerant ministry which marks the arrival of the Kingdom.

The conclusion to the scene picks up this connection and broadcasts it. Though the command to silence is a typical element from healing stories, an ironic twist develops. In contrast to this command, the victim 'preaches much' and 'announces the word'. As a result the crowds flock to Jesus. His work in the villages is hindered, but, as they did with John, the people flock to him in the wilderness.

A significant boundary has been crossed. A human declared unclean by the priestly religious code has been restored to medical, social and religious health. This restoration adds new lines to the character sketch of Jesus, whose authority is aimed at human restoration. In eradicating one boundary another is established: Jesus' ministry of word and deed will draw a solid line of demarcation between himself and the religious leadership of Israel.

Thus, a standard story form has been used once again to demonstrate the authority of Jesus' ministry. The literary details and the framing of this scene offer the reader further insight into the nature of Jesus and his work: its compassion, its divisive nature and its growing popularity.

Healing a Paralytic; Forgiveness of Sin (Mark 2.1-13)

Another type of boundary is faced in the stories from Mk 2.1-3.7a. While earlier scenes addressed the crisis of physical illness, demon possession and uncleanliness, these stories focus upon religious boundaries.

The scene in Mk 2.1-13 employs the conventions of a healing story to tell of a paralytic. The introduction brings Jesus and his associates to the scene. The gathering of the crowds is noted, and Jesus speaks 'the word' to them. The difficulty of the disease is demonstrated when the paralytic is born by four friends, but further complications are met when the crowd hinders their access to Jesus. The healing occurs through the command of Jesus (2.11), the healing is confirmed when the victim takes up the pallet and walks away and the acclamation of the crowd is noted. The story closes with the departure of Jesus and the crowds.

This formal pattern has been employed in an uncommon manner. The determination of the friends to bring the paralytic to Jesus is exemplified in the dramatic act of digging through the roof, and their persistence is characterized by Jesus as faith. Of key importance is the healing command: 'Child, your sins are forgiven you.' This statement is not unthinkable in a world-view where sin and sickness stand in close relationship, but this command initiates a distinct break in the story (2.6-10). This sidenote is filled with a debate between Jesus and the scribes over who can forgive sins. This theological concern functions in the story as an issue of characterization. 'Who is this that speaks thus?' ask the scribes, and they conclude that Jesus is a blasphemer. A different image is constructed around other elements of the story. Jesus knows in his spirit that they are questioning his authority and identity. A climactic focus is reached in 2.10 with the claim that the son of man has authority to forgive sins upon the earth. Precisely at this point comes the healing command.

While the plot line of this scene provides further demonstration of Jesus' power, this is not new. Demons have been cast out, sicknesses healed, lepers cleansed, and the form of the story is common. What is distinct about this scene is its concern for characterization and Christology—what it says about Jesus. The one who is able to heal broken bodies and minds is also able to enact God's forgiveness. His insight into the needs of the victim and the complaints of the scribes deepens his profile. The final claim of the story is dramatic: the son of man is authorized to offer God's forgiveness, and Jesus is that son of man. The acclamation of the crowd defines this event, and thus this characterization, as a new reality that serves to bring glory to God (2.12). The final lines of characterization are sketched in the closing: Jesus, the teacher, instructs the crowds beside the lake.

What is the reader to do with these claims? If the first reader takes part in Jewish piety, that reader knows the truth of the claim in 2.7: God alone forgives sin. The first reader also knows that God's forgiveness is announced and actualized through human figures such as Moses and the prophets. The reader also knows that pronouncing forgiveness of sin is a priestly task. The reader of the Old Testament may remember the priestly atonement liturgy in Leviticus 16 and the repeated formula of forgiveness (Lev. 4.26, 31, 35; 5.10, 13, 18; 6.7). While later generations perhaps believed that Jesus forgives sin, the first reader is left with a distinct claim wholly congruent with the theology of the Old Testament: Jesus, the son of man, is empowered to announce God's forgiveness for sinners.

Readers ancient and modern are left with puzzling questions. Chief among these is the meaning of the phrase 'son of man'. In the linguistic world of this Gospel 'son of man' may be a way of speaking of human beings in general. A case can be made that this phrase is a circumlocution—a way of speaking indirectly about one's own self. Within the New Testament the phrase may refer to a heavenly figure who will come at the end of the age. Within the Gospels the phrase 'son of man' comes to be used as a title that refers to Jesus. This scene does not solve the issue, and other scenes offer only partial explanation concerning this phrase. In addition to the ambiguity of the son of man title, other questions remain for the reader of this scene: How do sin and sickness relate? Has Jesus taken over the priestly functions for the people of Israel? The story does not pretend to solve all of these issues, and not all will be clarified by later events.

Nonetheless the scene in Mk 2.1-13 puts forward a stark new claim about Jesus—a claim witnessed by disciples, by crowds and by readers. Using a standard pattern for healing stories, the form is broken open by controversy and dialogue between Jesus and the scribes. At issue is God's forgiveness of sins. The scene, as now constructed, insists that God's forgiveness is available precisely in the work of Jesus, the son of man.

Another boundary has been crossed, this time in the realm of religious experience. Faith—even the faith of persistent friends—may be met by God's forgiveness. This forgiveness is available to one who has not yet asked, and this forgiveness is available in a house in Capernaum in the presence of Jesus.

Calling Sinners (Mark 2.13-17)

This scene realizes the crossing of another type of religious boundary—that separating the righteous and the sinner. While most of the previous scenes used the form of healing stories, the account of the paralytic was reshaped by the controversy at the heart of the scene. The story in Mk 2.13-17 employs the form of a controversy scene to narrate the debate over religious values. Thus a shift in both focus and form is under way.

The transition in 2.13 concludes the last scene and sets the stage for 2.14-17. In the story of Jesus the lake is a place of transition, but especially of instruction (4.1-2) and calling (1.17-20). Thus the activity of Jesus in 2.12-14 characterizes the nature of his work: he teaches the crowds and he calls disciples.

The call of Levi echoes the call of the fishers (1.17-20). Like them he is named and identified through his father. Like them he is characterized by his vocation. Like them Levi is given a stark invitation—'Follow me'— which he immediately obeys.

What would certainly distinguish this call for the first reader is the notation that Levi is a tax collector. The call of common fishers to a rabbinical pattern of discipleship is perhaps colourful, unexpected, intriguing, and it may create various strands of identification among common readers. But the call of a tax collector is shocking and provocative at a number of levels. From a political standpoint Levi is a traitor to his people, taking their taxes on commission and handing them over to their Roman captors. From a religious standpoint Levi is unclean, dealing with the dirty coins of Gentile landlords. From a sociological standpoint Levi represents a hated class of outcasts. That Jesus would call him as he called the fishers and that Levi would respond as they did is a shocking claim that the first reader would find hard to digest—unless, of course, the reader identifies with people like Levi.

In a pattern typical of this Gospel, the scandal is broadened and multiplied. Jesus reclines at the table with Levi in his (Levi's?) house. Through this identification a host of social and religious taboos are broken; either Jesus has joined Levi's group or Levi has joined Jesus' group. The scandal is multiplied by the note that many tax collectors and sinners joined them in this meal (1.15). The final commentary broadens the number of sinners and presents an ongoing association: 'they were many, and they were following him'.

This scandalous fellowship sets the stage for the controversy scene. The objection is embodied in the scribes of the Pharisees who witness these events. Their problem is with Jesus, but their questions are directed to the disciples. Here the historical setting of the literature pokes its head through the scene. The later followers of Jesus—like those first readers in the Markan community—must deal with the scandal of Jesus' work, and a primary line of debate continues between this community and their Jewish heritage.

The answer to the scene and to the reader is given in a pronouncement by Jesus. While some earlier scenes contained sayings by Jesus (2.10-11), this scene is built around the concluding pronouncement that decides the controversy. Using a parabolic image—'the healthy do not have need of a physician, but the sick do'—Jesus proclaims the nature of his own work: 'I have not come to call the righteous, but sinners.'

This controversy scene and its concluding pronouncement cross the religious boundary established between saints and sinners. The religious and the noncommitted are confronted by the shattering of taboos well established within the world of the text. This sign speaks to various levels of reading. At the historical level it exemplifies the ongoing conflict between Jesus and traditional forms of Jewish piety. At the level of the first reader it addresses the present tension between their Jewish heritage and their own social location in a world of sinners. The modern reader, for whom such social and religious distinctions may seem quaint, is reminded that the line between sacred and secular is forever under negotiation.

Through these literary transactions new dimensions are added to the portrait of Jesus. The authority demonstrated in the conflict with demons and disease and uncleanness is now turned to the religious boundaries separating out the sinners. Likewise the image of discipleship is stretched in new directions: among the many who hear his call and follow him are Levi and his kind.

Debating Religious Ritual (Mark 2.18-22)

The debate over religious boundaries continues. The interlocutors in this scene are the followers of John and of the Pharisees, and the issue is fasting. Fasting is presented as a normative expression of Jewish piety, even among the followers of John. The absence of fasting among the Jesus movement initiates the controversy. As in the prior scene the real debate is about the followers of Jesus—a question that remains relevant in the world of the first reader. As is typical of controversy scenes in this Gospel, a pronouncement by Jesus provides the solution. Drawing upon Jewish wedding traditions, Jesus employs parabolic images to address the question of fasting: the friends of the groom do not fast while the groom is at the feast. The image soon gives way to allegory: when the groom is taken way, seemingly against his will, then the friends of the groom may properly grieve. This dense imagery is followed by proverbial images: a new patch will not work on old clothes, and new wine will not work in old skins.

These images share a common message that goes well beyond the initial issue of fasting. Those who follow Jesus take part today in a fellowship of wondrous joy. Something new has come that old traditions cannot contain, and this wonder must be celebrated. In this way Jesus' eating and drinking with sinners is presented as the advent of a new time, and the reader should know that this is the time of the Kingdom. A boundary has been crossed between those who fast and those who feast, but a greater boundary has been crossed by those who follow Jesus into the new age of the Kingdom.

Debating The Law (Mark 2.23-28)

The stakes are higher in the controversy scene of 2.23-28. Here the boundaries set by the law of Moses are debated by Jesus and the Pharisees. The controversy centres around the actions of Jesus' disciples, who gather grain while passing through a field on the sabbath. The first reader knows that such work is forbidden on the sabbath day, and this objection is voiced by the Pharisees. As in previous scenes the issue centres around the disciples, but the answer is provided in a pronouncement by Jesus.

While the Pharisees draw upon the legal code of the covenant for their position (Exod. 31.13-17; 34.21), Jesus cites a story from 1 Sam. 21.1-7. Thus, both sides are citing Scripture in support of their position; one draws upon the authority of Moses, the other upon the authority of David. Jesus identifies the priest in the story as Abiathar, though 1 Samuel notes that Ahimelech is priest at the time. Later readers saw this mistake, and the name is omitted from a few later texts.

The Davidic story cited by Jesus shows that the bread on the altar is properly used to satisfy Israel's future king and those with him. The climactic pronouncement by Jesus shifts the issue of the bread to the larger matter raised by the Pharisees—proper observance of the sabbath. Moving from the details to the principle at stake in the scene, Jesus declares that 'the sabbath exists for humans, and not humans for the sabbath'. This principle shatters the Jewish legal boundary that separates sacred and secular, giving priority to human need. This principle is then interpreted through a 'son of man' saying: 'The son of man is master even of the sabbath.' If 'son of man' is understood in its common sense as a reference to a human being, then the final phrase is simply a restatement of Jesus' first pronouncement: the sabbath exists to serve human need. The first reader has already been encouraged to see 'son of man' as a title uniquely related to the identity of Jesus. If read in this way, a new dimension is added to the characterization of Jesus: the son of man may announce God's forgiveness (2.10), and the son of man is master of the sabbath (2.28).

However 'son of man' is understood—as human beings or as a distinct title for Jesus and his work—the priestly role is clear in both scenes. Pronouncing God's forgiveness and determining the use of the shewbread are both priestly tasks. These have now been taken over by the work of Jesus, in whose ministry the forgiveness of God and the joy of the sabbath are made available to human beings. Well-defined traditions, even the law of Moses, have been realigned, and the boundary between sacred and secular has been redefined. A stark line of controversy has been drawn between Jesus and the religious leaders of Israel. Those who follow Jesus observe these transitions and take part in this new experience.

Observing the Sabbath (Mark 3.1-7a)

The scene in 3.1-7a unites the focus on wondrous authority with the concern for religious boundaries. To accomplish this union the scene employs a mixed form drawn from healing stories and from controversy stories.

The introductory lines bring both concerns to the stage: the scene is set on the sabbath in the synagogue, a disabled person is present and Jesus is under observation. The pronouncement form takes over the centre of the story. While the victim is first addressed, the larger part of the pronouncement is addressed to the observers. The legalities of the sabbath provide the central focus, and two alternatives for working on the sabbath are posed by Jesus: doing good/saving life versus doing evil/ taking life. The confrontational speech of Jesus is met by the silence of his opponents. The posturing of Jesus ('looking about' and 'grieved with anger') contrasts the hardness of his opponents and the healing activity of Jesus.

The form returns to that of miracle stories with the healing command and the restoration of the hand. In the place of the expected acclamation and the spreading report, this scene ends with an ironic twist. Those who seek to preserve the sabbath now employ it as an occasion for working evil; sacred and political interests unite as they plot together with the Herodians to bring about the death of Jesus. As with other stories, the geographical transition of Jesus concludes the scene (3.7a).

In this way the scene in Mk 3.1-7a unites the developing line of Jesus' wondrous works and his debate with the religious authorities of Israel. This is accomplished by the mixing of two story forms (miracle and controversy), but also by the narration of multiple boundary crossings. The laws separating sabbath activity from common activity are breached and rewritten in order that Jesus might accomplish good for a wounded human. This double crossing is no accident, for it shows that Jesus' breach of traditional piety has its purpose in the overcoming of human bondage. A new twist emerges from this scene and casts its shadow across the pages of the Gospel: in his work of overcoming human sin and sickness and bondage Jesus violates the norms of traditional piety, and it is precisely this breach of faith that leads to the death plot.

The Story Thus Far

What does the reader know thus far? The setting shifts from scene to scene. Beginning in the wilderness and the Jordan river the story moves to the Lake of Galilee. The first sabbath is set in Capernaum, the only village named. From there the scenes convey the itinerant ministry of Jesus in the synagogues and houses and villages of the Galilee.

The plot line moves from the preaching of John to the baptism of Jesus and his subsequent trial in the wilderness. His ministry starts at the point where John's ends, and Jesus begins with the announcement that God's Kingdom is near. The pattern established on the first sabbath in Capernaum is cast across the whole of Jesus' work: the authority of his teaching is demonstrated in his wonders. This work breaks down the boundaries preventing full human existence: evil spirits, disease, uncleanness, sin, religious traditions and structures. At the same time, the work of Jesus in behalf of the Kingdom is marked by controversy with religious leaders and the first signs of his own suffering and death.

The initial patterns of characterization are in place. A small cast of named characters inhabits the world of the story: John the Baptist, Jesus, Simon, Andrew, James, John, Zebedee, Levi. Unnamed figures fill out the story: the crowds, the hired servants in Zebedee's boat, a man with an unclean spirit, Peter's mother-in-law, a leper, a paralytic and four friends, scribes, tax collectors, sinners, disciples of John, Pharisees, a disabled person, the Herodians. Most of these figures play a role within the story, but never develop into full characters: only the disciples and Jesus are subject to real development.

A key portrait of Jesus is under construction. Told in the opening lines that Jesus is the Christ and son of God, the reader is shown through various scenes the dimensions of Jesus' identity. Endowed with God's Spirit and endorsed by God's voice, Jesus' deeds in behalf of the Kingdom are marked by a new and wondrous authority. He is the teacher empowered to challenge the boundaries separating humans from the full life of God's Kingdom.

The disciples also show a developing profile. Five are called by name, identified by family and drawn from their previous tasks (1.16-20; 2.14). Disciples witness the teaching and healing activity of Jesus, and they share some private instruction (1.35-38). They are questioned by religious leaders (1.16) and are the focus of controversy in two scenes

(1.18; 1.23-24). These preliminary sketches show the disciples as witnesses, companions and participants in the ministry of Jesus.

Though unnamed, the image of the religious leaders is taking on traits of character. They observe the work of Jesus, inquire, question, debate and complain. By the end of this unit they have accused Jesus of blasphemy and plot his death.

The crowds also accompany Jesus, but their role is not yet clear. They are marked by curiosity (1.27) and amazement (1.22, 27), and they spread the report of Jesus' activity (1.28). Initial images of discipleship are also suggested: Jesus teaches the crowds beside the lake (2.13).

The reader is also developing a relationship with the narrator. While heavily involved in the opening lines, the voice of the narrator soon blends into the scenes. Showing takes priority over telling, and the narrator intrudes only to give information and cues to the reader.

Formal strategies are emerging. The stories of Mk 1.21-3.7a employ traditional story forms—exorcisms, healings, summaries, controversies—to show the work of Jesus. Significant changes found within these scenes bend the stories toward the question of Jesus' identity and toward the issue of discipleship. Two particular signs emerge from these stories: Jesus is the teacher whose authority is demonstrated in his deeds, and this teaching stirs controversy and opposition among some religious leaders.

What does this mean to the first reader? We can only guess. These scenes are likely selected and shaped to present the example of Jesus before a community of Galilean followers in the period around the first Jewish War (late 60s and early 70s). The emphasis on Jesus' conflict over traditional Jewish piety likely reflects the community and its debates with Jewish leaders in the Galilee. In Jesus' deeds they find an alternative to the traditions of the scribes and the Pharisees of their own day. In his movement among the villages and crowds of Galilee they find the source and the affirmation for their own work. In his overcoming of various boundaries they find the salvation and release which they identify with the new work of God's Kingdom. In the call of Jesus to Galilean fishers and tax collectors they hear their own call to follow him. This is, perhaps, what the story means to the first reader. What the story means to modern readers is yet to be seen, and this will be addressed at the end of the commentary.

Mark 3.7-6.6: Parables and Signs

Mark 3.7 begins a new act in the story of Jesus, yet the pattern is familiar. A glance at the outline of Mk 3.7-6.6 shows that it repeats the basic cycle of 1.21-3.7a. An opening summary of Jesus' work (3.7-12) is followed by a call to disciples (3.13-19). With notable authority Jesus teaches in various scenes throughout the Galilee. A scene of rejection (6.1-6) closes the section.

When a narrative repeats itself in this way, several explanations are possible. One explanation is that repetition shows incompetence on the part of the narrator. This pattern may also say something about the competence of the implied readers: that the narrator thinks they have not yet comprehended the message and need to hear it again. A third explanation may be found in much ancient literature: cycles are repeated to reinforce the experience of the reader, but also to add new dimensions to a familiar pattern. The Gospel of Mark is replete with examples of this pattern of repetition and development. The passion prediction is given on three occasions (8.31; 9.31; 10.32-34), but significant differences emerge from the three sayings. Three cycles of prayer are found in the scene at Gethsemane (14.32-42), but a progression is evident. This pattern of repetition and development may breed familiarity and boredom; if done properly, this technique alerts the reader that something old should be seen in a new way. This pattern is frequent in classical music, where a common phrase or theme is reprised in multiple variations. This technique most likely comes from an oral strategy of presentation, but it has been taken over into the written presentation of this Gospel. The reader is invited to listen again, as if for the first time. Thus Mk 3.7-6.6 revisits the earlier ministry, reinforces it basic patterns, and adds new dimensions to the character and work of Jesus.

Staking Out the Work of Jesus (Mark 3.7-12)

This new act begins with a gathering of the people. As the crowd flocks to Jesus beside the lake, the reader is reminded of the opening sketch of John the Baptist (Mk 1.4-8): from all of Judaea and from Jerusalem the people flock to the Jordan to hear John. A similar account is given of Jesus' activity: in the first act (1.21-3.7a) the report of Jesus goes throughout the Galilee (1.28, 45), and great crowds gather (1.33; 2.1-2, 13). In this new act (3.7-6.6) Jesus draws a more diverse audience to the lake: they come from the Galilee, from Judaea and from Jerusalem, but also from Idumaea, from across the Jordan and from Tyre and Sidon (3.7-8). While the preaching of John called people from Jewish regions to repentance and baptism, this new movement to Jesus (3.7-12) exceeds the traditional bounds of Judaism. The gathering in Mk 3.7-8 thus repeats a theme familiar from the first act, but, for the attentive listener, important new dimensions are present. The localized ministry of John's preaching has been extended in the deeds of Jesus; crowds come from as far south as Idumaea, from as far north as the Phoenician city of Sidon, from as far west as the Transjordan. At the core of this gathering is a large group from the Galilee who are following Jesus; this emphasis on following suggests a growing band of disciples. The size and enthusiasm of the gathering is emphasized in the possibility that the rush of the crowd will become dangerous and oppressive (3.9).

A similar pattern of reinforcement and development is found in the report of Jesus' activity. The summary in Mk 3.10-12 encapsulates the miracles of the previous cycle (1.21–3.7a). Jesus heals many people, and he casts out demons from others. Like the crowd in Capernaum (1.32-33; 2.1) and the four friends (2.1-12), these people are eager to be near Jesus and to experience his healing touch (3.10). As in earlier stories the exorcized spirits cry out and are commanded to silence (3.11-12). Repetition of these familiar themes reinforces the characterization established earlier: the wondrous deeds of Jesus break through oppressive boundaries and demonstrate the authority of his teaching.

More importantly, this repetition brings new depth to the theme. In the previous cycle Jesus healed by touching (1.31, 41); here the sick press upon Jesus in order to touch him and be healed. The new dimension is the suggestion that even a passive touch from Jesus may heal. Also new to this scene is the focus on falling before Jesus. The crowds press Jesus or 'fall upon' him (3.10), and this imagery is extended in the action of the possessed: they 'fall before' him (3.11). In a similar way the response of the demons is intensified. Previously they are silenced in their attempt to identify Jesus (1.25, 34). The demons who do cry out identify him ambiguously as 'the Holy One of God' (1.24). A more direct confession escapes in this scene: 'You are the son of God' (2.12). Jesus rebukes them, lest this identity become known (3.12).

These variations upon the opening cycle create both connection and advancement. The work of Jesus continues in this new section, but with interesting and important nuances. The reader knows from the opening lines of the Gospel that Jesus is the son of God, but now demons threaten to broadcast this news. The crowds who follow Jesus are growing in number, in diversity and in intensity. A new stage is unfolding in the story of Jesus' mission and identity.

Calling the Twelve (Mark 3.13-19)

Like the first cycle (1.21-3.7a), this section has an opening call to disciples. Continuity exists between this scene and Mk 1.16-20. Like James and John (1.20), these people 'go away' when Jesus calls (3.13). As in 1.16-20, James and John as well as Peter and Andrew are called. As in the earlier scene, disciples are sometimes identified by their family or by their activity (3.17-19).

While the pattern is familiar, key variations are present in this second calling scene. First, the number has increased from four to twelve. There are more followers in the second scene, and the first reader may see in the number 12 a symbol for the tribes of Israel.

Secondly, the identity of various individuals is highlighted. Simon has been renamed as Peter, and James and John have been designated the 'sons of thunder' (3.16-17). Another James is described as the son of Alphaeus, another Simon is designated as 'the Kananaion', which may mean he is a Zealot. Judas is identified by his family or his place of origin (Iskariot). The notation that Judas is the one who betrayed Jesus is a prospective flashback that reflects the point of view of the reader rather than the time of the story. This intrusion not only sharpens the identification of Judas; it also warns the reader about a key moment in the upcoming story. An ironic context is established: at the moment the closest followers of Jesus are established, the reader knows that one of them will cause his downfall.

Thirdly, the task of disciples is given closer analysis. The narrator tells that the Twelve will also be known as 'apostles' (1.14), and the first reader knows that this means 'ones who are sent'. This new title is clarified in the description of their tasks: they are to be with Jesus, and they are to be sent out by him (3.14). The goal of this sending is further defined: they are to preach and to exercise authority over demons (3.14-15).

Fourthly, this scene describes a new direction for the calling. In 1.16-20 James and John 'go away' after Jesus, and the four follow Jesus. In 3.13-19 Jesus goes to a mountain from which he calls disciples. The reader who knows the Old Testament might remember stories, like those of Moses or Elijah, in which the mountain is a place of God's instruction and revelation. The conscious choice of Jesus is emphasized—he calls whom he chooses—whereas the first calling seems almost by chance. In 3.13-19 the first direction of following is to 'go away' to Jesus, and the first task of discipleship is to 'be with him'.

Even as the opening story (3.7-12) specifies and intensifies the identity of Jesus, so this scene broadens the parameters of discipleship. Four fishers have become twelve apostles, and they are to occupy a unique place in the story of Jesus.

Other Responses to Jesus (Mark 3.20-22)

Even as the second act expands the scope of Jesus' ministry and of his followers, so the opposition to Jesus is given new dimensions. In the first act (1.21–3.7a) crowds pressed upon Jesus with wonder and awe, while opposition to Jesus came from unclean spirits and from some religious leaders. In this act the crowds press more urgently, taking away the opportunity to eat (3.20). The circle of controversy widens and the opposition intensifies. 'Those with Jesus' likely refers to family or friends or followers. Believing Jesus to be beside himself, they come to take him away (3.21). Scribes from Jerusalem accuse Jesus of being possessed by the devil, and they credit his power to cast out demons to his collusion with the ruler of demons.

The Teaching Ministry (Mark 3.23-35)

The pattern of expanding and developing Jesus' identity, his followers and his opposition in the second act of the Gospel carries over to the teaching ministry. Whereas Jesus' teaching of the Kingdom centred first in his wondrous deeds, the second act also demonstrates the power of a his language. This includes explanation of a new form: the parable. While parabolic language was heard in the first act (2.19-22), the second act will develop a theory of parables in connection with the teaching of Jesus (4.10-12).

The first parable emerges without explanation and with no clear description of the audience. The question addressed by the parable arises from the charge of the scribes in 3.22—that Jesus casts out demons by the power of the ruler of the demons. 'How is Satan able to cast out Satan?' asks Jesus. He then offers a parabolic reply to his question: a kingdom or a house or Satan cannot endure internal warfare. In contrast to the scribes' theory of internal division in the house of Satan, Jesus offers an alternative: the turmoil in the house is due to the entrance of an external power that is stronger. The significance of the parable is clear: Jesus casts out demons not through collusion with Satan, but because he has plundered Satan's house and kingdom.

The first act also witnessed Jesus' teaching through pronouncements (1.27), and this form is given further development in the second act. The pronouncement of Jesus in 3.28-29 defines two levels of sin: humans may be forgiven all sins except for blasphemy against the Holy Spirit. The first reader likely finds this saying as confusing as the modern reader. The 'sons of men' phrase in 3.28 refers to humans and not to Jesus as the son of man. In the Gospel of Mark no theology of the Holy Spirit has emerged. What is the reader to do with this charge? The attentive reader knows that the Spirit descends upon Jesus at his baptism (1.10) and that demons recognize him as 'the Holy One of God' (2.24). The reader knows about the temptation by Satan in the wilderness (1.13) and that it is the Spirit who drives Jesus to this testing (1.12). The reader also knows the charge that Jesus is crazy (3.21) and that he is in collusion with the leader of the unclean spirits (3.22). Thus the reader is in a position to know that the saying in 3.28-29 draws upon this evidence and upon the parable of 3.23-27 to define the spiritual power of Jesus. To reject the spiritual power of Jesus is to reject the power of the Spirit given at his baptism and to reject the one who anointed him; there is no release from this sin. Lest readers, ancient and modern, fail to follow this circuitous logic, the narrator intrudes to make the connection: this pronouncement is given 'because they were saying he has an unclean spirit' (3.30).

This development of teaching and controversy continues in 3.31-35. The mother of Jesus and his brothers come to the house where he teaches, they stand outside and they send word to him. The reader knows from 3.21 that tension exists between Jesus and those close to him. The call of his relatives provides the occasion for a new form of teaching: the leading question. 'Who is my mother and my brother?' Jesus asks the crowd seated around him, raising the suspicion that he indeed has lost touch with reality. The answer is a clear parabolic image of discipleship: those who follow Jesus, attend his teaching and do the will of God compose his true family. In one short sketch the reader is introduced to a different style of teaching, to a new level of controversy and to new dimensions of discipleship.

The attentive reader may also note a transition in setting. From the lakeside (3.7) and the boat (3.9) and the mountain (3.13), Jesus now goes to 'the house' (3.20). Multiple variations upon this image can be seen to surround Jesus' teaching. His former household think him crazy and come to take him away (3.21, 31). He is accused of collusion in the 'house' of Satan ('house' appears four times in 3.25-27). In contrast to these images of rejection, Jesus finds in the crowd who press upon him and sit around him in the house a new family of disciples. This image of the house as a place of instruction set in contrast to the rejection of Jesus elsewhere will be developed in the upcoming stories.

A Cycle of Parables (Mark 4.1-34)

Jesus' teaching in parables is fully developed in Mk 4.1-34. An introduction and conclusion (4.1-2, 33-34) mark off this unit, four parabolic units demonstrate his teaching, and an explanation of how parables work is provided (4.10-12). This is a teaching unit. The plot line pauses, with no real action in this episode. The setting is stable, with only the transition from the lakeside to being alone with the disciples (4.1-2, 10). The only characters who speak in these episodes are Jesus and the disciples. The voice of the narrator is subtle. As a consequence the attention of the narrative falls wholly upon the role of parables in the teaching ministry of Jesus.

The cycle of parables opens with an introduction that connects the cycle to previous teaching, defines the audience and provides the setting. As before, Jesus teaches beside the lake and is pressed by the people. Teaching from a boat, Jesus addresses the crowds in parables.

The opening word is 'Hear!' The first reader may remember that the central teaching of Moses opens with this call: 'Hear, O Israel, the Lord our God is one Lord' (Deut. 6.4). The first reader will also know that such hearing is not just auditory, but always involves obedience. What follows is a short parable in which a single character repeats the act of sowing under various conditions. The failure of this planting beside the way, on the rocky soil, on the shallow soil and among the thorns is contrasted by the amazing productivity of the good soil. The parable closes as it began, with a call to hear (4.9).

This brief and colourful image drawn from common scenes typifies the teaching of Jesus. This parable fits well with what the reader knows of Jesus' story thus far. The parable embodies in a new form the previous scenes of Jesus' ministry. Jesus has come forth into the land of the Galilee announcing that God's Reign has drawn near. He has met various forms of tension and opposition: from Satan in the wilderness; from crowds who press upon him and limit his activity; from those near him who think him crazy; perhaps from his family; from unclean spirits; from the Herodians; from religious leaders who question and grumble, who accuse him of blasphemy and of collusion with Satan, who plot his death. Standing in contrast to this difficulty is the productivity of Jesus' work: the sick are healed, lepers cleansed, demoniacs released; disciples leave their work and follow him; crowds attend to his teaching; faith grows among his hearers (2.5). On the difficult soil of the Galilee the gospel of the Kingdom is taking root. The parable thus speaks directly to the nature of the Kingdom and to the situation of those who are following Jesus in his own day.

The interpretation that follows the parable (4.10-20) encourages the reader to see the flexibility of such stories: they speak not only to the time of Jesus, but also to the current situation of the reader. This is modelled in the private interpretation given to the Twelve and others with Jesus (4.10). To those who are with Jesus the mysteries of the parables are unfolded, and this instruction has to do with the Kingdom of God. Thus the parable is made effective not only in the context of Jesus' work in the Galilee, but also in the lives of later followers. Through this strategy the first readers, and all readers, are encouraged to apply the teachings of Jesus for their own questions, their own context. Mark 4.10-12 has as much to do with the general nature of the parables as with the content of the specific parable from 4.3-9. Though enigmatic, the parables of Jesus partake in the coming of the Kingdom of God, and these teachings are given for all who go with Jesus.

This expansive pattern of interpretation and application also has a negative side. Those who are outside, those who do not draw near to Jesus, will find his teachings enigmatic. Apart from the context of the Kingdom and the call to discipleship that Jesus issues, these lessons remain ineffective. A new pattern of 'in and out' has been established. While the expected division is between Israel as the chosen people of God and Gentiles as outsiders, Mk 4.12 is cited from Isa. 6.9 and refers to Israel's failure. Failure to see and hear the message from God prevents repentance and healing. It is significant that this division now occurs around the teaching of Jesus.

Those who follow with Jesus are in danger of missing this message, so they require a further word of interpretation (4.13). An allegory of types follows (4.14-20). Various elements of the story are identified with real-life counterparts: the seed is the word; the birds represent Satan; the sun represents tribulation and persecution; the thorns represent the cares of this age, delight in riches, and other desires; the different soils represent various types of hearers.

Thus, the reader is confronted by two stages of the parable. The first recitation (4.3-9) offers a brief story with a warning to listen, but with no explanation of its elements. This parable is given to those who are beside the lake. Its images are directly applicable to the events of Jesus' ministry as told in the previous scenes. The focus of the story is the amazing productivity of the seed, despite the difficulty of the landscape.

A second reading of the parable (4.13-20) is directed toward those around Jesus and with the Twelve (4.10). This interpretation connects the story directly to the enigma of God's Kingdom. Using allegorical typology, the second reading is focused upon the reception of the word and the responsibility of the listener, and it creates a new definition of insiders and outsiders.

The reader is thus informed of a hermeneutic for the parables. While they are available as historical events for a general audience, these stories remain meaningful only in connection with the call to the Kingdom, with discipleship in the path of Jesus and with participation in the community of his followers. Any reading from 'outside' this context will remain enigmatic. The careful reader will soon realize that this hermeneutic will not be repeated, and no other interpretation of individual parables will be offered. The enigmatic stories that follow must be taken up by those who choose to hear. Their connection to the Kingdom must be revealed for each reader as a mystery connected to their own discipleship within the community of Jesus' followers. In this way the parables, which emerge from Jesus' proclamation of the Kingdom, are imported into the world of the reader to guide the quest for discipleship.

As in the change from the first act (1.21–3.7a) to the second act (3.7–6.6), the transition from the first reading of this parable to the second reading demonstrates how familiar stories may be read in new ways. The first reading offers encouragement for all who spread the word of the Kingdom. Through trying times and difficult terrain, the reader is encouraged to persist. Though rejected by most, when the message is received it proves to be productive beyond all logic or expectation. Be careful how you sow, warns the first reading, for the Kingdom grows in surprising ways from difficult circumstances.

The same story offers a different message in the second reading. Be careful how you hear, says this reading, lest the word prove unfruitful in your life. This sequence demonstrates that the parables are polyphonic: they speak with different voices to different hearers and to different ages. This hermeneutic of flexibility insures the relevance of these stories, and thus their endurance. The parables of Jesus are set forth as enigmatic treasures that must be discovered anew by an unending line of readers.

What follows in Mk 4.21-25 is, strictly speaking, not parabolic. These images are metaphorical in function, but they are given in the form of pronouncements. Their connection to the previous lesson on parables (4.1-20) is found in their illustrative nature. Like the parables, these colourful pronouncements are taken from common life and illuminate the life of the Kingdom. Mark 4.21-25 appears to assemble a string of pronouncements or wise sayings that are only loosely related. Their connection is found in a pattern of word linkage in which a concept from one saying occasions another saying. This likely represents an oral

pattern of collection that has been put into writing. The following para-
phrase shows the flow of this sayings sequence:

Saying 1: No one lights a lamp then hides its light.
           (hiding)
Saying 2: There is nothing hidden or secret that will not be revealed.
           (making known)
Saying 3: Listen!
           (listening)
Saying 4: Look at your listening!
           (the basket of Saying 1, one form of measure)
Saying 5: You will be measured as you measure, and more added.
           (adding)
Saying 6: Those who have will be added to; those who have not will be
           subtracted from.

While such sayings are typical of the way Jesus taught and were scattered throughout his ministry, this Gospel collects these pronouncements and places them in connection with the parables and their reading strategy. Thus the reader is encouraged to see in these pronouncements a further word about the mystery of the Kingdom. Following the
hermeneutic of the parables, the reader is to find the sense of these
sayings in the fellowship of Jesus and in the way of discipleship. The
warning in 4.24 ('See how you hear!') echoes the verdict of 4.12, taken
from Isaiah 6 ('Seeing, they see and do not understand, and hearing, they
hear and do not comprehend'). The reader is encouraged and warned to
heed these words as a part of the secret to God's Kingdom.

The story in Mk 4.26-29 is technically not a parable, but a simile. In
the introductory line that 'the Kingdom of God is like a person who
might scatter seed upon the soil...' the reader should recognize a variation of the parable of the sower from 4.3-9 and its second reading in
4.13-20. Thus, a familiar story is given a new application. This new
account tells nothing other than the natural process of planting and
growing and harvesting, though the wonder of growth is noted. Because
of the connection to the parable theory (4.10-11), the reader is to see in
this natural sequence an image of the Kingdom: small seeds grow in
wondrous ways and lead to a fruitful harvest. Here the connection to the
Kingdom is explicit (4.26).

Another simile for the Kingdom is found in 4.30-32. The parallelism of
4.30 ('How shall I compare...and in what parable shall I put it?') shows
that this simile is considered as a type of parable. Again the connection
to the Kingdom is explicit: 'How shall I compare the Kingdom of God?'
(4.30). The reader should see here a fourth version of the sower: when a
tiny mustard seed is sown it grows into a large shrub. Various terms

echo the first reading from 4.3-9: sowing, the earth or soil, the springing up of the seed, the birds.

Thus Mk 4.3-32 presents four variations upon an agricultural image in order to illuminate the arrival of God's Reign. The first reading (4.3-9) emphasizes the difficult nature of the task, but also the amazing result. The second reading (4.13-20) is offered as an insider appropriation of the first reading and emphasizes the importance of one's receptivity to the message. The third variation (4.26-29) uses the normal growing season as an image of the Kingdom. The sequence of development is emphasized, as is the intrinsic nature of this growth. The final variation (4.30-32) repeats this growth sequence but emphasizes the development from microscopic origins to greatness.

In this manner Mk 4.3-32 demonstrates its own theory of parables. Each reading is connected to the larger story of Jesus, who goes about the Galilee teaching with authority. The connection of this teaching to the imminent Reign of God is made clear and is demonstrated in various literary patterns. The diversity of the form is shown in the variety of materials described as parabolic. The flexibility of the form is demonstrated in the multiple variations of the sower story. The interpretative matrix for such stories is spelled out in 4.10-12 and demonstrated in the narration of the various parables. The reader is left with a model and guide for reading further accounts of Jesus' teaching through story; these accounts are to be read and re-read as images of the Kingdom that can be properly understood only in connection with the work of Jesus, only in the task of following Jesus, and only in the community of Jesus.

As Mk 4.33-34 indicates, this discernment is a process still underway. In many such 'parables' the disciples will be offered 'the word' as they are able to hear. The understanding of this teaching is a part of the fellowship of Jesus with his followers (4.34). In the story that is unfolding—and in the life of the reader—the mystery of the Kingdom is to be found.

Commanding the Storm (Mark 4.35-41)

The static setting of the teaching scene (4.1-34) gives way to transition and to action. New attention is given to the deeds of Jesus and to the boundaries they cross. The pattern of the story in 4.35-41 is familiar to the reader of this Gospel: after a geographical transition the problem or opponent is presented, the nature of the threat is demonstrated, a command from the wonder worker addresses the situation, wonder and acclamation follow, a final transition (5.1) leads to the next scene. While the first reader may know similar stories from Jewish and Greek tradition, earlier scenes in the Gospel of Mark also use this form to demonstrate Jesus' wonders. Because a familiar pattern has developed, the reader is invited to notice both the similarities and the differences in this story.

The notice that Jesus intends to go to 'the other side' (4.35) may signal not only transition, but a change in environment. Previous experience in this Gospel suggests a boundary crossing is imminent.

One element is incongruent with the traditional form of the story. In the midst of the threat disciples cry out to Jesus as 'Teacher' (4.38). This title seems odd in a storm story, where something like 'Master' or 'Saviour' would seem more relevant. Teaching would normally be associated with words of wisdom rather than wondrous deeds. The teacher title is probably at odds with the genre of this story, but it is precisely aligned with the theology of this Gospel. The connection established between Jesus' teaching and his wonders in Mk 1.21-39 is taken up into this story. He who is heard by the wind and the waves is the Teacher who seeks to call out faithful discipleship from his followers.

Earlier opposition to Jesus appeared in the form of sickness or unclean spirits or accusing religious leaders. Here the opponent is a natural phenomenon, but the language of exorcism is used. The waves are 'thrown upon' the boat, and this term is similar to the word describing the 'casting out' of demons. A similar image is present in Jesus' response. He 'rebukes' the storm, which is the same word used to confront demons (1.25, later of Peter/Satan in 8.33). Jesus' words to the storm—'Silence, be muzzled'—also echo the exorcism scenes: demons are not permitted to speak (1.34; 3.12), and the command to 'be muzzled' is used against unclean spirits (1.25). The calming of the storm is thus presented as a type of exorcism aimed at nature itself. This intensified form of exorcism fits well in the world of the first reader, where sea and storm stories abound with images of darkness, chaos and evil (Gen. 1.1-10; Exod. 14; Ps. 104.5-9; Job 27.20-23; 41.1-11; Jon. 1).

While this story intensifies the power of the threat, and thus the wonder of the resolution, another pattern is also at work. Despite the intensity of the storm and its images, a greater threat is present. The command of Jesus stills the storm, but the fear and faithlessness of the disciples remain. 'Why are you cowardly?' Jesus asks, 'Do you not yet have faith?' (4.40). The fear of the disciples (4.41) points in two directions. Such fear is the proper response to an epiphany—the experience of the divine presence (Exod. 3.6). In this scene, however, the fear of the disciples is indicative of cowardice and unbelief. The acclamation is similarly reshaped: usually offered as a sign of wonder, the question of the disciples—'Who is this...?'—seems inappropriate for those who have witnessed the deeds of Jesus.

Thus a familiar scene offers important new images, particularly in terms of characterization. The calming of the storm presents a fortified exorcism story and demonstrates anew the authority of Jesus. The real crisis, however, is found in the hearts of the disciples, who fail in understanding, faith and courage. What should be an epiphanic moment marked by acclamation becomes instead a scene of fear and confusion. While the storm is silenced in this scene, the fear of the disciples rages on.

Among the Gerasenes (Mark 5.1-21)

The exorcism in Mk 5.1-21 employs the elements expected in such stories. A transition brings Jesus onto the stage (5.1); he is confronted by a difficult case of possession (5.2-8); the demons are expelled through his command (5.8, 13); there is a demonstration of the healing (5.14-16); the miracle is accompanied by awe and acclamation (5.15-16); the report of the deed is spread (5.14, 20); Jesus departs to another scene (5.21a).

This performance of a recognizable story form encourages the reader to notice variations, developments and nuances in the expected pattern, and there are many in this scene. Since 4.35 Jesus has been headed for 'the other side', and he reaches this new environment in 5.1. The approach by a man with an unclean spirit echoes the scene in 1.21-28. Various parallels encourage the reader to continue this comparison: both victims are described as 'a man with an unclean spirit'; both are violent; both 'cry out'; their cry to Jesus, given in broken grammar, is remarkably similar ('What to us and to you...?' in 1.24; 'What to me and to you...?' in 5.24); typical of demoniacs, both recognize Jesus and seek to name him (1.24; 5.7); both fear torment at the hands of Jesus (1.24; 5.7); both offer lofty descriptions of Jesus which border on confessions ('Jesus Nazarene...the Holy One of God' in 1.24; 'Jesus son of God Most High' in 5.7). These connections encourage the reader to see the scene in Mk 5.1-21 not only as variation of the traditional story form, but specifically as a second reading of the exorcism in 1.21-28.

This mirroring technique creates a host of developments, and these enlargements prove important to the plot line, to the growing lines of characterization and to the larger set of signs created by this Gospel. A contrast in setting is developed along the lines of Jewish/Gentile distinctions. The first scene was set in Capernaum in the Galilee, while the second is set in the Gentile region of the Gerasenes. This boundary crossing is confirmed in the description of the victim: in 1.21-28 the victim is found in the Jewish synagogue, while 5.1-21 draws the victim from an unclean origin—the tombs of the dead. This regional contrast is developed along further lines. In terms of Jewish piety this is an unclean region; it is inhabited not only by mobs of unclean spirits, but also by Gentiles who keep unclean animals. Ultimately Jesus is unwelcome in this land (5.17).

This mirroring effect involves not only contrast, but also intensification. The description of the problem in 5.2-13 is extensive and dramatic, far exceeding that of 1.21-28. The victim of 5.1-21 is possessed by a mob of unclean spirits and names himself as Legion. This designation may also recall the violent Gentiles who occupy Palestine—the Roman legion of soldiers. The description of Legion's activity intensifies the portrait: he lives among the dead, he cannot be subdued or chained, he lacerates himself, by night and day he screams among the tombs and mountains.

Not only the description, but also the effect of the demons is intensified. In 1.21-28 the demon 'tears' the victim, then 'cries out' as it departs. In 5.1-21 the demons beg not to be tortured, then ask to be sent into the unclean swine who inhabit the region. Their evil is revealed in a final scene of violence: unclean spirits enter unclean swine, then plunge to their death. The waters of the lake, with their images of threat and chaos (4.35-41), swallow up the spirits.

This pattern of intensification is seen also in the demonstration of the cure. While the cure was described in one verse in the first story (1.26), the second story elicits witnesses who observe Legion clothed and in his right mind (5.14-17), then narrates a conversation between Jesus and Legion (5.18-19).

The acclamation and spread of the first story throughout the Galilee (1.28) is paralleled by the spread of the report in the city (5.14) and throughout the region of Decapolis (5.20). The final line of intensification is seen in the response of Legion, who seeks to follow Jesus and is then sent to 'preach' in his own home and in the region of Decapolis (5.18-20).

Mark 5.1-21 thus offers to the alert reader a stark development upon the theme established in the sabbath at Capernaum. There Jesus' teaching authority was demonstrated in his power to enter into the realm of unclean spirits and release its victims. This scene is re-enacted with significant intensification among the Gerasenes. Having crossed the turbulent waters (4.35-41), Jesus disembarks on 'the other side'. He enters a land abounding in unclean images: mobs of demons running naked among the tombs and mountains, grazing swine who serve as their host and rush to their death in the waters, inhabitants who are fearful and inhospitable. A mass exorcism ensues, and the scene becomes a regional event. A new level has been reached in the characterization of Jesus and in the demonstration of his power.

This pattern of mirroring and intensification lends its most dramatic effect to the characterization of those who follow Jesus. While the fishers (1.16-20) and Levi (2.14) leave all to go with Jesus and the Twelve are called to a special role (3.13-19), the failure of those who follow Jesus becomes evident. 'Those with him' think him crazy (3.21); there seems to be tension between Jesus and his family (3.31-35); the disciples do not understand the parables (4.10-13); the storm reveals their cowardice, lack of faith and fear (4.35-41). A growing line of characterization is developing around the failure of those who follow Jesus.

In contrast to this theme Legion asks to be with Jesus—a clear image of discipleship (3.14; 5.18). Echoing the 'house' images that surround Jesus' instruction to his followers (1.29; 3.20), Legion is sent to his own house to tell what he experienced (5.19). While other exorcisms end with a command to silence, 5.1-21 ends with Legion's report to his own people. Most significantly, Legion 'preaches' through the Decapolis, and in doing so he fulfils the task of disciples (3.14-15).

As a result of these literary moves the pattern of boundary crossing established in the first act of Jesus' ministry (1.21–3.7a) is carried forward in dramatic fashion, and important lines of characterization are developed. Jesus, who teaches throughout the Galilee with deeds of wonder and words of wisdom, now crosses the boundary separating Jews from Gentiles. This crossing produces an epiphanic moment of revelation, but it also unveils the failure of Jesus' followers. Dramatic narrative images portray the land of the Gerasenes as evil, insane, unclean, inhospitable. Jesus' excursion into this region provides a mass exorcism in which mobs of demons and herds of pigs flee into the depths of the lake. At the end of the scene the transformation is complete and a new preaching mission is under way. Now clothed and in his right mind, Legion preaches the story of Jesus through the region of the Decapolis. The work of Jesus has been carried into new territory with an amazing result.

A Tale of Two Daughters (Mark 5.21-43)

Mark 5.21-43 presents one complex episode composed of two distinct miracle stories. The whole unit is framed by the movement of Jesus. He returns to the Jewish side of the lake in 5.1, then moves to his hometown in 6.1. The notice that Jairus is a ruler of the synagogue (5.22) confirms a return to a Jewish setting. The first story tells of the healing of a 12-year-old daughter of the ruler of the synagogue. A common pattern is seen again: Jesus moves onto the scene; the need is presented, with particular difficulties noted; the healing is accomplished with a touch and a command; the reality of the raising is demonstrated when the daughter walks and is to be given food; a command to silence is given; Jesus moves on. New developments may be found within this familiar pattern.

This story is unusual because the victim is rarely present and never speaks or acts in the story. The illness of the daughter is reported by the father. The confidence of the father in the power of Jesus is also extraordinary: 'Come and place your hands upon her so that she might be saved and might live' (5.23). Jesus seeks to sustain this faith in the face of the daughter's death: 'Do not fear, only believe' (5.36).

This story is unusual not only for the absence of the victim and the persistence of her advocate, but also for the difficulty encountered. Jesus must journey to the house of the daughter, and his travel is interrupted (5.25-34). The death of the daughter is then reported to Jesus (5.35). When he arrives at the daughter's home, Jesus is met by a tumult and by weeping and wailing. His words to the mourners are met with laughter (5.40).

Another unusual element is the description of Jesus as 'the Teacher' (5.35). As in previous scenes this designation seems foreign to the genre but quite at home in the developing theology of this Gospel.

The most significant difference in this story is that it involves raising the dead. Thus the pattern of repetition and intensification of miracle stories throughout the second act (3.7-6.6) culminates in this scene.

Read sequentially, this story has been interrupted by a second story (5.25-34). This intrusive scene narrates a different healing. The pattern of this story is also familiar: a victim approaches Jesus; her illness is described, noting the difficulties involved; a touch from Jesus accomplishes the healing; she is dismissed by Jesus.

Several variations within this story are noteworthy. It is the woman who approaches Jesus in this scene, and the healing touch is at her initiative. The automatic nature of the healing is also noteworthy. More significant is the extended conversation between Jesus and the victim. This type of exchange was first present with Legion's conversation on discipleship (5.18-19). Here the topic is salvation, and the blessing of Jesus upon this woman is a new element for the Gospel. 'Daughter, your faith has saved you', says Jesus. 'Go up in peace and be made well from your sickness' (5.34).

The nature of the illness also reshapes the story form. The woman is described as 'being in a flow of blood 12 years', a condition not responsive to medical treatment. This condition is typically understood as a chronic haemorrhage from her womb, though this is unrealistic. A more probable explanation is that she has experienced her menstrual cycle without interruption for 12 years; she has not been able to conceive, and this creates a crisis within her social framework. Whatever the problem is, the healing cannot be demonstrated within the confines of the story, so this usual element is missing.

The real power of this episode emerges from a technique not yet seen in the Gospel of Mark: the intertwining of two stories to create a distinct episode. The healing of Jairus' daughter has been broken open (5.22-24, 35-43), and the story of the woman with the flow of blood has been inserted (5.25-34). This intercalation creates a mirroring pattern in which one story interprets the other, inviting the reader to explore new connections and new dynamics set in motion by this relationship.

The linking of these stories creates a bond between the two victims. The first is a 'daughter' (5.23, 35) of 12 years (5.42) who needs to be 'saved' (5.23). She has an advocate—a father of power and reputation who falls before Jesus to openly present her need (5.23-24). The opponent that threatens her is a terminal illness. The second victim is also a 'daughter' (5.34), and she has been sick for 12 years. She too needs to be 'saved' (5.28), and Jesus accomplishes this for her (5.34). All her helpers prove costly, but useless (5.26), and she has no advocate to plead her cause. Instead she approaches Jesus in the crowd and touches his garment. When she is discovered, she falls before Jesus and presents her own need. The disease that threatens her is chronic, but not terminal. The two victims are not only affected physically; they are each rendered ritually unclean by their disease. The healing of the two daughters is marked by fear (5.33, 36), but also by faith (5.34, 36). Thus, the two victims create a mirroring effect in which the story of each impacts the story of the other.

The mirroring of these two characters generates important twists in the plotting of the episode. First, the intercalation creates a sense of narrative time. The use of the journey concept and the insertion of the second line of action occupy the reader and provide a sense of the passage of time. The narrative movement from the opening motif in 5.21 to the closing movement in 6.1 is a long and arduous journey. In addition to the departure provided by the internal story (5.25-34), the plot line is marked by intrusions and diversions of various sorts. Two settings and three audiences are required to accommodate the wanderings of the story, and the narrator intrudes periodically into the plotted action.

Although this technique of narrative retardation may produce boredom, it also provides narrative tension and expectation. The reader suspects the destination of the story but does not know when these expectations might be fulfilled. Each delay creates a sense of foreboding and urgency, and the death of the daughter confirms this danger. Indeed, one daughter seems to have been sacrificed in the interest of the other, and the initial plot line seems destined to end in death and failure. Thus, the plot movement and expectation of the first line of action come to a halt with the death of the daughter. Only through a complex series of moves and an unparalleled miracle scene is the victim reached and saved. This delay and misdirection creates narrative tension and expectation, and it highlights the reversal that resolves the tragedy.

This narrative strategy also creates a pattern of reinforcement. The mirroring of traits, needs, destinies provides a pattern of mutual reinforcement. What is known to be true of one story can be suspected to be true of the other. A sense of foreshadowing and fulfilment is created, reinforcing the values of the narrative.

The third effect of juxtaposing the two victims is narrative intensification. While the two units mirror and reinforce each other, definite trends of intensification are at work. These stories move by levels. The presentation of the need moves from a reported sickness (5.23) to an actual sickness (5.25-26) to a reported death (5.35) to the presence of the dead one (5.38-40). The display of power moves from the report of Jesus' power (5.27) to an inadvertent display (5.29-30) to the raising of the dead (5.41-42). This intensification of need and power is accompanied by a growing level of secrecy. Jesus dismisses the first audience (5.37), then the second audience (5.40), leaving only three disciples and the parents to witness the raising. Finally even these witnesses are commanded to silence (5.43), leaving only the narrator and the reader as witnesses to these events. This process of intensification of need, power and secrecy magnifies the climactic moment in which the dead daughter is raised.

The final narrative effect from the juxtapositioning of these stories is that of narrative focusing. The sense of retardation, expectation and intensification focuses the plot action around the raising of the dead daughter. Her need is more dramatic, as is the act of power that meets that need. Thus, the plot action finds its centre in the raising story.

While the focus of the plot action belongs to the raising, the ideological focus lies in the response of the woman with the issue of blood. The daughter of Jairus is a ficelle—a flat, one-trait character—known only in terms of her need. In contrast to her passivity the approach and response of the other victim is dynamic and colourful. The woman with the issue of blood plots her healing out of desperation, rumour and hope (5.25-28). She presents herself at the feet of Jesus in a posture of reverence (5.33). Jesus defines her response as faith—a faith that saves her, makes her whole and gives her peace (5.34). While all response to the raising is silenced, the faith of the other woman is praised, and she is sent on her way in peace. In this way the woman with the flow of blood models the ideal response to Jesus and his authority.

These four major plot developments result from the intercalation of the two stories and the mirroring of their characters. The impact of this relationship is profound. While the authority of Jesus has been extended to its limits in the raising of the dead daughter, the impact of this characterization is limited. Constrained to silence, the ideological focus falls upon a different part of the story. Prior to the raising, Jesus is cast again as one who teaches with authority (5.21), and from within this characterization both healings occur. In a similar way, new light is shed on the role of discipleship. In the presence of the powerful teacher sent from God, the proper response is not simply awe, but reverential fear and obedient faith (5.33-34). This experience with a new literary pattern— intercalation—schools the reader in the hermeneutic of this Gospel. Because of this encounter the reader is alerted to the nuance and the dynamics of subsequent intercalations.

The pattern of boundary crossing continues. Through his wondrous deeds the Teacher (5.35) has traversed the border between the living and the dead. More importantly perhaps, an unclean woman tormented by chronic illness has crossed the boundary into faith, wholeness, peace and salvation.

Going Home (Mark 6.1-6)

Even as the first act (1.21–3.7a) closes with a death plot, the second act of this Gospel (3.7-6.6) closes with a story of rejection (6.1-6). The alert reader will also note the parallels with the scene at Capernaum that opened the first act (1.21-39). Both scenes are set in a familiar village (Capernaum in 1.21; Nazareth? in 6.1); disciples accompany Jesus in both stories; both are set in the synagogue and emphasize Jesus' teaching; the crowds in both stories are amazed at his teaching and question the source of his authority.

These similarities create a narrative frame for Jesus' ministry. What began on a sabbath in Capernaum (1.21-39) has spread through the Galilee. Jesus has traversed the land announcing the Kingdom of God, casting out demons, healing the sick. Through the repetition and development of familiar story forms, the demonstration of his power grows in intensity, as do his character sketch and the profile of those who follow him. The hometown scene in 6.1-6 brings the second act (3.7-6.6) to a close by returning to these roots.

Because of this framing of the ministry of Jesus, the homecoming event of 6.1-6 stands at a crucial junction of the story and carries key interpretative weight. The basic image of Jesus is confirmed: he journeys through the Galilee, followed by disciples. His teaching in the synagogues is met with awe and wonder. As in the first act (1.21-3.7), the crowds are amazed at Jesus' wonders (6.2). New twists are also added: the recognition of Jesus' 'wisdom' reflects developments in the second act that highlight the power of his words (3.23-30; 4.1-34).

An extraordinary new development is found in the rejection that meets Jesus in this scene. While he has faced hostile religious leaders, fearful and slow disciples, inhospitable Gentiles, sceptical companions (3.21), Jesus is met here with a new level of resistance. What the crowds know of Jesus' work is contrasted with what they know of his origins, and these hearers are 'scandalized' (6.3). The alert reader will recall the parable of the sower. In the second reading of this story (4.15-20) the seed sown on rocky soil represents those who hear the word and receive it with joy. These, however, do not have roots, and they are temporary. When difficulties arise because of 'the word' these hearers are 'scandalized' (4.16-17). Such awe mixed with offence is found in the hometown scene of 6.1-6, and this image provides a closing commentary on the ministry of Jesus.

The final words of the act belong to Jesus, and this pronouncement offers one key to his identity. Jesus, like the prophets of old, is honoured everywhere except in his hometown, among his relatives and in his house (6.4). The reader is to perceive in the image of the rejected prophet a new and dramatic profile; hints of this characterization were found earlier (3.6; 5.17), but its full dimensions will be developed in upcoming scenes.

A crescendo develops through the first two acts (1.21-3.7a; 3.7-6.6) around the theme of Jesus' authority. He has called disciples, cast out demons, healed the sick, cleansed lepers, offered God's forgiveness, calmed the storm, performed a mass exorcism, raised the dead. This wondrous authority is shown to be a trait of his role as the Teacher (1.22; 4.38; 5.35). The second act thus ends with an amazing observation by the narrator: confronted by the lack of faith in his hometown, Jesus is unable to do any miracles. This absence is not from lack of power, for the narrator observes that Jesus' powers are intact (6.5). This absence of miracles is explained in the ironic claim of 6.6: while observers are typically amazed at Jesus' powers (1.22, 27; 2.12; 4.41), here Jesus is amazed at their unbelief (6.6).

Thus, the crescendo of power and authority crashes in the synagogue scene in Jesus' hometown (6.1-6). The building image of Jesus' power nurtures a growing concern for the connection between faith and healing (4.40; 5.23, 34, 36); sometimes faith is part of the healing. The opposite connection is demonstrated in 6.1-6: unbelief explains the absence of miracles. The power of Jesus is able to cross over various boundaries separating humans from God's wholeness, but not that of unbelief.

The Story Thus Far

Building on themes and patterns from the first act of Jesus' ministry (1.21-3.7a), Mk 3.7-6.6 brings new episodes to the story of Jesus and new dimensions to his profile. The settings centre again in the villages and synagogues of the Galilee and alongside the lake, but the reach of Jesus' ministry is extended. Followers now come from Judaea and Jerusalem, but also from Idumaea, from across the Jordan and from Tyre and Sidon. Jesus himself traverses the lake to the 'other side', he confronts the Gerasenes and his work is taken throughout the Decapolis.

New settings emerge. From the mountainside Jesus calls the Twelve and defines their mission (3.13-19). From the boat he instructs the crowds (4.1). A contrast in setting develops around Jesus' ministry of instruction. He teaches the crowds in the villages and synagogues and beside the lake; private instruction is given to his closest followers in 'the house'.

New characters are added to the cast. Many are flat, one-trait images who serve a function with the story. The daughter of Jairus (5.21-24, 35-43) is never named, never acts and never speaks. The woman with the flow of blood (5.25-34) is not named, but her responses and experiences are paradigmatic. Jairus fills the role of persevering advocate (5.21-24, 35-43). Legion (5.1-21) represents a host of demons, but also a model for discipleship. The Twelve are named, their backgrounds described and their mission defined (3.13-19). Group characterizations abound. 'Those with Jesus' (3.21) think him crazy and come to take him away. His family calls for him (3.31), and they are mentioned in the scene of rejection (6.1-6). Gerasenes (5.1-21) fear Jesus and wish him gone. Jerusalem scribes accuse Jesus of collusion with Beelzeboul (3.22). Crowds press upon him, listen to his instruction, stand in awe at his deeds.

Two patterns control the plot line. First, familiar stories are told in new ways. The ministry of Jesus develops within expanding circles of influence. The circle of Jesus' followers grows in number and in assignment. The miracle stories of the second act gain new intensity and nuance, and their role in the characterization of Jesus becomes evident. The stories of two daughters are intertwined (5.21-43), creating complex patterns of plotting, characterization and focus. The second plotting pattern involves a pause in the line of action. Within these periods Jesus offers public and private instruction to his followers.

Important steps are taken in the characterization of Jesus. His call to the Twelve from the mountainside suggests a connection to the work of Moses. His sending of Legion (5.18-20) confirms Jesus' authority. His power is demonstrated with growing drama and intensity, progressing from the stilling of the storm to a mass exorcism to the raising of the dead. His ability as a wonder worker is unsurpassed, but the most significant demonstration of his power lies in his ability to call forth faith and wholeness (5.34, 36). The connection of these wonders to his role as the Teacher is reasserted (4.38; 5.35). His teaching authority finds a new dimension in the wisdom of his words (3.23-35; 4.1-34; 6.2). Signs of compassion (5.36, 43) and creativity (4.1) emerge. His prophetic role is revealed (6.4) amid growing resistance and rejection. His reticence for public display and his resistance to notoriety become evident. Through these literary transactions the profile of Jesus is taking on subtle nuances and dramatic depth.

The characterization of those who follow Jesus also undergoes changes in the second act. Apostles are named, and a wider circle of disciples emerges. Colourful characters confront Jesus and demand his attention. A more diverse crowd follows with curiosity and fear. The second act (3.7-6.6) develops the theme of failed discipleship. 'Those with Jesus' (3.21) think him crazy, and tension seems to develop around his family (3.31-35). Disciples are filled with fear and cowardice, and they do not yet have faith (4.40-41). They do not understand his parables, and they need further instruction (4.10-13).

The opponents of Jesus also take on new dimensions. Scribes think him an ally of Satan (3.22). He is unwelcome among the Gerasenes (5.17) and rejected in his hometown (6.1-6).

The second act of Jesus' ministry (3.7-6.6) engages the reader at a new level. New literary forms are employed. Subtle variations upon old patterns are given. New techniques of interpretation are offered. Subtle guidance and helpful information are provided by the narrator. The challenge of unfolding the teachings of Jesus in new settings is placed before the reader.

The crossing of boundaries continues in the story of Jesus. The call to the Kingdom is extended to a wider circle of followers. Some of these are women, some are Gerasenes. The parables define new terms of 'insider' and 'outsider' around the teachings of Jesus. The chaos of nature is stilled. An excursion is made into the unclean region of the Gerasenes, those on the 'other side'. A mass exorcism is performed, and a new follower is claimed from tombs. The line separating Jews and

Gentiles is breached. A dead daughter is returned to the land of the living, and a wounded daughter is released unto faith, salvation, wholeness and peace. The most difficult boundary has not yet been fully crossed, for the faith and courage of discipleship cannot be compelled.

Through these literary transactions the Gospel of Mark builds a growing set of signs. In Jesus' ministry the Reign of God stands near. The power demonstrated in his words and deeds is sufficient to cross all boundaries separating humans from the full life of the Kingdom. Unexpected and uninvited guests are finding their way to this salvation, but the way of Jesus and the way of discipleship proffers difficulty, controversy, rejection. For the Kingdom of God and its messenger, the ground is both fertile and rocky.

Mark 6.6b–8.27a: Beyond the Borders

The third act of this Gospel (6.6b–8.27) repeats the patterns established in the previous acts, but dramatic developments are under way. As in the previous acts, this cycle opens with a notice of Jesus' ministry (1.14-15; 3.7-12; 6.6b) and with his call to disciples (1.16-20; 3.13-19; 6.7-13). As with previous cycles, this act opens and closes with the movement of Jesus (1.16; 3.7a; 6.6b; 8.27a). Familiar forms will inhabit this cycle: a call to disciples, miracles stories, teaching scenes. What is distinct about this act has more to do with its focus than with its content. The nature of discipleship is re-examined in this unit, and the role of the Gentiles is considered. These two themes are merged, and contrasting lines of characterization develop. Those expected to follow Jesus meet with difficulty while unexpected followers respond to his ministry. Thus the reader is invited in this act to revisit familiar territory in order to see more clearly the nature of Jesus' work and the demands upon those who would follow him.

Jesus' Ministry of Teaching (Mark 6.6b)

Jesus' ministry is marked by his travels throughout the Galilee, teaching in the synagogues and villages. The authority of his teaching is demonstrated in the wondrous acts through which he drives back forces that constrain human life, but also in the wisdom of his words. This itinerant ministry of word and deed announces the nearness of God's reign and offers the first signs of its arrival. The reader who has listened well to the previous stories knows this. The opening lines of the third act (6.6b-8.27a) provide a summary statement that serves as a reprise, sounding again the major chords of Jesus' ministry. The alert reader should know the import of this summary: Jesus travels through the surrounding villages, and a new cycle of ministry has begun.

Calling the Twelve; The Death of John (Mark 6.7-31)

As in the previous acts (1.16-20; 3.13-19), this cycle opens with the calling of the disciples. The progression in the description of the disciples and their role continues in this third calling. Here the Twelve are sent out by Jesus in pairs and are given authority over unclean spirits (6.7). Beyond this, a new approach is defined. The outfit for disciples is described: they are to travel without food or bag or money, and they are to take only a staff, sandals and a single garment (6.9). A new strategy is given: they are to stay in the first house they enter, and they are to perform a prophetic sign (shaking the dust from their sandals) against those who reject them (6.10-11). The result of their mission is given: they preach repentance, they cast out demons and they heal (6.12-13). At the end of the scene the disciples return as 'apostles' and report on their work and teaching (6.30). They are invited to share with Jesus a time of retreat from their busy activity (6.31).

The advance in the identity and work of the disciples becomes evident. The Twelve have been established in their following of Jesus (3.14, 16); now they realize the work for which they were called (3.14-15). Their independence is established when they are paired and sent out on their own. More importantly they go out and do what Jesus has done (1.39). A greater development has occurred: the response to the disciples and their message has become determinative for the people who hear them. Their mission and message stands, in essence, in the place of Jesus. Even as Jesus sent the healed leper as a witness against the high priests (1.44), so the disciples offer a witness against those who reject the message—and the messengers—sent by Jesus. The Twelve have thus been elevated to a decisive role in the arrival of God's Kingdom; through their ministry the work of Jesus is multiplied and is broadcast to the villages of the Galilee.

The reader who gains familiarity with the style and strategy of this Gospel will recognize here a second case of intercalation. As in 5.21-43, two stories have been intertwined. Here the mission of the disciples (6.7-13, 30-31) is broken open, and the death of the Baptist (6.14-29) is narrated in the midst of their mission. The effect of this literary pattern upon the telling of the story and upon its images is dramatic.

From a literary perspective the intervention of the Baptist story creates the passage of time. Rather than showing the result of the mission immediately, an interim period is created, and the reader understands that the Twelve are at work. This pattern of delay gives a durative sense to the story of the Twelve, and the report in 6.30-31 seems timely.

Beyond this temporal reorientation, the reader has learned that intercalated stories interpret each other. The work of John is thus cast in the role of discipleship. Long before the sending of the Twelve, John also preached repentance (1.4). His work is cast in the light of their work.

More significantly, the work of the Twelve is cast under the shadow of John. He came forth preaching. He enacted his message in his appearance and his way of life. He was imprisoned, and now he dies for his work. Jesus has come forth in the steps of John, announcing the Reign of God and demanding repentance (1.14-15). He has encountered opposition and rejection, and there is a death plot under way (3.6). Now the Twelve are sent to preach repentance and to embody the message of Jesus. The alert reader will see the connection. Like John, Jesus will give his life, then the disciples will follow in his path. These subtle connections foreshadow the way ahead, and they link the destiny of John to that of Jesus and his followers.

The sober account of John's death (6.14-29), serves not only as a backdrop for the work of the Twelve; it also completes the characterization of the Baptist. John is defined in this Gospel through five scenes. In the opening scene (1.2-7) John stands as the renewal of the prophetic voice, calling Israel to repentance. Included in his message is the recognition that John's ministry will be followed by that of the 'greater one' and his baptism in water followed by that of the Spirit (1.7-8). In the second scene (1.9-11) John is the baptizer of Jesus. The third portrait of John is found in the opening lines of Jesus' ministry: 'After the imprisonment of John, Jesus came into the Galilee preaching...' (1.14). The longest description of John is found in the interlude scene of Mk 6.14-29. Further mention of John occurs at Caesaraea Philippi (8.28), where some speculate that Jesus is a revived John. A final description is found in 9.13, where John is described by Jesus as the returned Elijah who was put to death.

When the sending of the Twelve (6.7-13) is complete, the scene shifts abruptly to the inner world of Herod. Hearing of Jesus, Herod presumes that John has risen from the dead (6.14). Here the reader first learns of the death of the Baptist. The powers of Jesus stir various lines of speculation about his identity: he is Elijah or one of the prophets. Herod is certain, however, that this wonder-working prophet marks the reappearance of John. From these lines the reader also learns that John was beheaded (6.16).

The details behind this stark announcement are given in the scene that follows. Here the reader is not only given insight into the private world of Herod, but this information is provided in the form of a flashback that recalls the events leading to the present speculation.

The reason for John's imprisonment is explained—he criticized the marriage of Herod—and bold new lines are added to the character portrait of John. Herodias, wife of Herod, wishes him dead. Herod knows John to be 'a just and holy man', so he protects him. Herod is puzzled by his prophetic critic, but he hears him gladly.

The cause of John's death is narrated in 6.21-26. The leading citizens of the Galilee are entertained at the birthday of Herod. When the daughter of Herodias pleases the guests with her dancing, Herod vows to give her what she asks. Under the advice of Herodias, the daughter asks for the head of John. Herod is forced to choose between breaking his oath before his guests or taking the life of his prisoner.

The event of John's death is narrated with sombre brevity (6.27-29). John is beheaded in prison, his head is given to Herodias and his body is given to his followers.

Through this interlude the reader has learned much about John: he was imprisoned because of his moral preachments; he has drawn the ire of Herodias; he is recognized as holy and just; he sustains an intriguing relationship with Herod; his execution provided entertainment for the leaders of the Galilee; he has followers who are bold enough to claim his body.

John has thus preceded Jesus in proclamation, in imprisonment and now in execution. The shadow of John's story falls upon the one he baptized, for Jesus is seen in the image of John (6.14-16; 8.28). The characterization of John as the righteous prophet who suffers as God's messenger provides the pattern for the story of Jesus and casts its shadow over the mission of the disciples. This connection is made clear by the intertwining of the mission of the Twelve with John's execution. The death of John closes the internal flashback, and the scene returns to the Twelve (6.30-31). The scenery has changed, but the image remains.

Bread in the Desert (Mark 6.32-46)

The scene in Mk 6.32-46 adds a new miracle form to the repertoire of this Gospel—the feeding story. This story also brings new elements to the characterization of Jesus and his followers. The format of the feeding story is similar to other miracles: movement of the miracle worker opens the scene (6.32-34); a need is identified by a third party (6.35-36); the difficulty of the problem is demonstrated (6.37); the wondrous act is accomplished (6.41-42); a confirmation of the wonder is provided (6.43-44); movement closes the scene (6.45-46). Such stories of gift miracles are known in the world of the first reader.

This scene points the reader in two directions. While similar stories may be known from their own day, the reader is also encouraged to see here various Old Testament connections. Even as Moses fed Israel in the wilderness during the exodus (Exod. 16.13-15), so Jesus, in a desert place, feeds his followers. Even as Moses divided the people in subgroups to provide for their care (Num. 2.1-34), so Jesus does (6.39). The mention of 12 baskets may allude to the 12 tribes. The image of green grass (Ps. 23) and the citation from Numbers 27 (found in 6.34) develop the image of Jesus as shepherd for God's flock. New lines are thus added to the focus on Jesus' identity and work. He is now portrayed as God's shepherd who, like Moses, will guide God's people. The power of his leadership is confirmed in the feeding miracle. A new component is found in the compassion of Jesus (6.34). The story ends with a scene of prayer on the mountainside, evoking Old Testament images of revelation and calling.

A unique connection is reaffirmed in 6.34. Here the people take over the role usually occupied by the victim. The need of the people is established through an Old Testament citation: they are like sheep without a shepherd. The first response of Jesus to that need is unexpected: he teaches them may things (6.34). The Gospel of Mark thus establishes a primary need among God's people that is met through Jesus' work as teacher. The literary pattern is clear for the alert reader: in this Gospel the wonders of Jesus are demonstrations of his power to teach, and it is this ministry of instruction that most meets the needs of the people. This literary transaction accomplishes much. Rather typical miracle stories have been reoriented away from their magical overtones in order to establish a distinct portrait of Jesus. He is the Teacher in whose words and deeds the Reign of God is realized for the people of Israel.

The image of the people as a shepherdless flock sets the stage for further characterization of Jesus, but it also emphasizes the failure of Israel's leadership. Even as the healed leper bore witness to the impotence of the high priest (1.44), so the shepherdless flock testifies to the failure of Israel's leaders. The compassion and power of Jesus provides leadership, instruction and nourishment for God's people—a task left undone by the religious leaders.

The plotting of this scene is unusual, and these changes provide a clue to the significance of the story. The crowds, as the shepherdless flock of God, stand in the place of the victim. Their need is met at the first level by the teaching of Jesus, then on a second level by the feeding. Little attention is given to how the miracle occurs. The centre of the story is occupied by a dialogical triangle: the disciples become the agents through whom the work of Jesus for the crowd is accomplished. The expected acclamation of the miracle is replaced by a scene of prayer.

In this way a standard form of miracle story contributes unusual dimensions to this Gospel. Drawing upon Old Testament imagery and language, Jesus is shown to be the Shepherd and Teacher of God's people. The power and compassion of his ministry stand in stark contrast to that of Israel's leaders, and the followers of Jesus play a key role in the completion of this ministry among the people.

Through these techniques vital connections are established with the larger story. The Kingdom of God announced in Mk 1.14-15 is actuated in the calling forth of a new community to be the people of God. The wondrous teaching ministry established in Mk 1.21-39 and developed in subsequent scenes provides the basis of this calling. Disciples, called in Mk 1.16-20 and sent out in 3.13-19, participate in this new reality. In addition, the active role of the disciples points beyond this story to the world of subsequent readers.

An Appearance Scene (Mark 6.47-53)

The scene in Mk 6.47-53 employs a typical form for miracle stories, but it makes important alterations to that form. While most miracle stories in this Gospel open with the arrival of Jesus, this scene begins with his absence. To accomplish this the narrator intrudes into the story to provide the setting: evening has come, the boat with the disciples is in the midst of the lake, but Jesus is alone on the land. Building on the notice of 6.46 that Jesus is praying, this unusual technique starts the scene with the absence of Jesus—a motif that is central to the story.

The miracle form is altered in another important way. While previous miracles centred around exorcisms, healings, calming the storm, raising the dead or providing food, this scene takes the form of an appearance story. An alert reader would recognize that this scene is similar to Old Testament epiphany stories in which Yahweh appears to a human. The image of the storm is common to such stories, and the language of 'passing by' is sometimes used to narrate an appearance of Yahweh (Exod. 33.19, 22; 34.5-7; 1 Kgs 19.11). In addition, the use of the phrase 'I am' in 6.50 echoes the name of God and reflects the dialogue between Moses and Yahweh in Exod. 3.13-22.

This scene is also reminiscent of the resurrection appearance stories found elsewhere in the New Testament. The resurrection appearance in John 21 shares numerous similarities with this scene: the story begins at night; Jesus is on the shore, while disciples are in a boat on the lake; hearing his voice, they recognize Jesus; bread plays a role in both stories. Motifs from Mk 6.47-53 are found in other resurrection appearances. The Emmaus story in Lk. 24.13-35 also involves a struggle to recognize Jesus, as well as the bread motif. In the appearance story of Lk. 24.36-49 the disciples think Jesus is a ghost, as in Mk 6.49.

Thus, Mk 6.47-53 alters the form employed in miracle stories to focus upon the absence of Jesus and to create an appearance scene. Although this story tells of the appearance of Jesus rather than Yahweh, it shares the ethos of Old Testament epiphany stories. Although this scene occurs in the midst of Jesus' ministry, it shares the outlook of resurrection appearances. This imagery proves particularly dramatic in the midst of a

Gospel noted for its human portrait of Jesus and for its lack of resurrection appearances.

One other alteration proves crucial for the significance of this story. In most miracle stories the need is found in the presence of demons or sickness or death. Here the need seems, at first reading, to be found in the wind and darkness. Unlike the calming of the storm in Mk 4.35-41, Jesus does not speak to the wind in this story. He speaks instead to the disciples: 'Be courageous. I am. Do not be afraid' (6.50). In this story the fear and cowardice of the disciples is the real problem, and even the calming of the wind does not solve this need (6.52). While fear in the presence of an epiphany is expected, their fear is related to their failure to understand and to the hardness of their hearts.

Thus, a miracle story has been used to add something new to the characterization of Jesus. Through the images of epiphany and the use of 'I am', Jesus is revealed as the one in whom the power of Yahweh is uniquely at work. This revelation stands in stark contrast to the fear and misunderstanding of his followers. This story speaks especially to the first readers of this Gospel who, in the absence of Jesus, now experience the tumultuous era surrounding the fall of the temple. Within the world of the Gospel this scene offers a stark reminder and warning: while Jesus has crossed numerous boundaries separating humans from the full life of the Kingdom, he is not yet able to overcome the fear and misunderstanding that grip the hearts of his followers.

A Summary of Miracle Activity (Mark 6.53-56)

The scene in Mk 6.53-56 represents another variant on the miracle story form. While the landing in 6.53 provides the typical entrance of the miracle worker, no departure is narrated. Of more importance is the treatment of the miracle activity itself. More attention is given to the efforts of the people to bring the sick to Jesus (6.54-56b). Only the closing phrase of 6.56c actually tells of healing activity, and it does so in summary fashion.

Because of these alterations the scene serves as a generalization and summary of Jesus' activity. More so than other stories, this summary draws upon a primitive view of miracle activity: the people hope that touching the garment of Jesus will cure them. While the use of the term 'to be saved' is typical of healing activity, the reader is invited to see here a double meaning that includes both physical and spiritual health.

An important component of this story is the energy and creativity of those who seek healing. Those who recognize Jesus run throughout the region and bring the sick on cots. When Jesus enters into a town or a village or even a field, they place the sick before him and call out for help. They believe that even a passive touch from his garment may heal them. Thus this story emphasizes the hindrances that the sick must overcome to reach Jesus and the extraordinary measures they, and those who help them, take to cross those boundaries.

When seen in the context of the larger Gospel story this summary takes on new significance. The arrival of God's Reign is realized in the proclamation and teaching of Jesus. The authority of his teaching is demonstrated in his wondrous deeds. These deeds overcome the boundaries separating humans from God and create a new community under God's care. Scenes such as 6.53-56 in which the people stream to Jesus for healing demonstrate that these boundaries have been crossed and the formation of a new people of God is under way.

Teaching about the Law (Mark 7.1-23)

The second act of this Gospel shows Jesus moving from one setting to another: the villages surrounding Nazareth (6.6); in a desert place (6.32); on the mountain (6.46); on the lake (6.48); in Gennesareth (6.53); in the villages and towns and fields (6.56). In light of this movement, the pause in 7.1-23 is rather dramatic. Where Jesus usually goes to another place, here the Pharisees and the scribes come to him (7.1). Three different audiences are addressed: the religious leaders (7.1-13); the crowd (7.14-16); the disciples (7.17-23).

While the Gospel of Mark emphasizes that Jesus is one who teaches with authority and connects this authority with the coming of God's Kingdom, rarely does this Gospel show the content of Jesus' teaching. The unusual specificity of 7.1-23 points to the importance of this material, particularly for those who read this Gospel. While the issues raised have to do with the details of Jewish Law, the answers given by Jesus have to do with larger principles for understanding God's will.

The problem is posed in 7.1-2: Pharisees and scribes note that some of Jesus' followers are eating bread with unwashed hands. Such concern may seem strange to the first reader in a world with limited knowledge of hygiene. Apart from the question of hygiene, which is never raised here, the concern would also seem strange to a modern reader. Thus the narrator intrudes in an unusual way to explain this custom (7.3-4). The term that describes the washing may mean 'with care', or it may mean 'up to the elbow'. If the latter is true, the practice of washing is more ritual than hygienic. The narrator also notes the motivation for the custom: they are observing the tradition of the elders. There is also a social dimension to this custom: they always wash before eating after returning from the marketplace. The narrator cites this as typical of a much larger tradition of washing: they wash wine cups, drinking vessels, copper utensils and, in some texts, their beds! The comment by the narrator not only explains that the washing is ritualistic, but this intrusion also characterizes the washing as trivial and typical. Thus the narrator's comment helps to clarify—or to create—a polemical context for the scene.

The question is put in a unique way. Not the actions of Jesus, but those of his disciples are contested (7.5). By not washing their hands they show disdain for the traditions of their Jewish elders. This query sets the stage for an extended response by Jesus (7.6-13). This response is noteworthy because it provides a rare demonstration of the way Jesus interprets and applies the Old Testament. This instruction is also noteworthy for its heated, accusatory tone. Finally, this response is unique in that it never addresses the specific issue raised by the religious leaders.

Addressing the religious leaders as hypocrites (meaning actors), Jesus applies to them the scathing prophecy of Isa. 29.13, where Israel is accused of false worship. The major charge is levelled by Jesus in his own words: leaving the commandment of God, they observe human tradition (7.8-9, 13). He cites one example: the reinterpretation of the principle of *corban*, which gives obligations to God priority over those to parents. For Jesus this one example is typical of the way his opponents interpret and apply God's law. There is no explanation of how this relates specifically to the custom of handwashing.

Jesus turns from the religious leaders to address the crowd. The tone is urgent and imperative: they are called to Jesus and commanded to hear and understand (7.14). His instruction to the crowd is reduced to a single principle: being clean or unclean has nothing to do with what one eats, but with what comes out of a person. While this principle applies to a host of food laws, its relation to the issue of washing is unclear.

The third audience is addressed in 7.17-23. Here Jesus enters into the house, a place of private instruction in this Gospel. There the disciples ask about the parable. This might strike the reader as strange, since no true parabolic form has been used. Reference is apparently made to the saying on clean/unclean. The frustrated tone continues: 'Then are you also without understanding? Do you not know…?' (7.18). The remainder of the passage is given to an explanation of the saying from 7.15: a person is clean or unclean not because of what they put into the mouth, but because of the things that come out of the person.

This teaching passage seems to contain more heat than light, and it hardly addresses the specific issue raised by the Pharisees and the scribes. What is a reader to make of this?

First, this unit reflects an ongoing controversy within Judaism over how one is to do God's will. The conflict may have some geographical base, pitting Jerusalem against the Galilee. This conflict likely has social and cultural dimensions, pitting the religious establishment of Jerusalem against rural peasants of the Galilee. This aspect may be reflected in the view that the marketplace makes one unclean. The staging ground for this conflict is the religious tradition of Israel. Jesus' disciples are accused of abandoning the tradition of the elders; Jesus in turn accuses the leaders of abandoning the law of Moses and invokes the scorn of the prophets. This scene represents two Jewish perspectives on what it means to be faithful.

Secondly, the issue of washing of hands (7.1-2, 5) is a secondary one. The concern with kosher food laws is given more discussion than the issue of washing. The saying at the end of v. 19 may declare all foods clean, though it may refer to elimination of all foods from the body. Both concerns are secondary, however, to the main focus of this passage, which is how one interprets and applies the commands of God. This passage intends to demonstrate the hermeneutic of Jesus. He accuses the religious leaders of a reductionistic, legalistic approach to the law; they trivialize it through casuistry and thus avoid its demands. In contrast to their approach Jesus cites the prophet Isaiah and the teachings of Moses, then offers his own application of food laws. The reader does not have access to the leaders' view of Jesus.

Thirdly, this passage exposes the ethic of the Jesus movement. Righteousness before God is determined not by what one eats (and presumably how one eats), but by what comes from the inner person. The external problem of dirty hands holds no weight against the list of vices that come from inside (mulling over evil, immorality, theft, murder, adultery, greed, malice, deceit, indecency, envy—literally, the evil eye—slander, arrogance, folly). These issues echo the ten commandments, and they are given priority. Ethics, not eating, provides the standard for clean and unclean in Jesus' teaching.

Most importantly, this conflict is not about Jesus, but about his followers. The conduct of Jesus is never questioned, but his followers are the focus of both the charge (7.1-2, 5) and the instruction (7.17-23). Thus the story of Jesus has been used to answer a question facing the community of Jesus in later years. The community that lives by this Gospel must clarify its relation to the wider heritage of Israel, to the law of Moses, to the prophets, to the traditions of the elders. This debate is not simply a rhetorical matter; the conflict is a live issue between Jews who are seeking to find their way in the aftermath of the fall of Jerusalem. Over against the Jerusalem establishment and ritual expressions of piety, this community frames its own understanding of righteousness. To do so it draws upon the teaching of Jesus, and it claims for its own the commandments of Moses and the energy of the prophets. In doing so this community stakes out its own claim to the faith of Israel.

Apart from its role in the life of the reading community, this passage adds important dimensions to the portrait of Jesus and to his story. Previously Jesus was shown to be the authoritative teacher who announces, in word and deed, the coming of God's Kingdom. This passage gives unusual focus to the content of Jesus' teaching and characterizes him in the best of rabbinical tradition: he is able to argue from the Scriptures and to draw out the relevance of the law and the Prophets for his followers. The Kingdom that he proclaims breaks through the limits of social elitism, trivial legalism and empty ritualism. An important component is also added to the story line. The conflict between Jesus and religious authorities has been heightened, the debate has been centred around issues of Jewish identity and the authorities from Jerusalem have been drawn into the conflict. These new elements will be played out fully in the passion story.

Dealing with a Gentile Woman (Mark 7.24-31)

The movement of Jesus begins anew in this scene, and he crosses into the Gentile territory of Tyre. In addition to this geographical note, the desire of Jesus for privacy sets the ideological tone of the story.

The healing of the daughter of the Syro-Phoenician woman is told according to a standard form. The story opens and closes with the movement of Jesus (7.24, 31); the need is presented, then met. What is unusual about the story, compared with others, is its lack of an acclamation of the deed. More significantly, the victim is here represented by another. At the heart of this scene is a dialogue between Jesus and the representative, and this dialogue provides the ideological centre of this account.

The healing event becomes a secondary part of the story: the victim is never present, the healing occurs at a distance and no acclamation or broadcasting of the healing is shown. The scene is dominated by the controversial dialogue between Jesus and the woman and by the pronouncements that come from this exchange. Thus, a typical form has been stretched into a new shape.

The response of Jesus to the woman's request for healing fits coherently into the world-view of first-century Judaism: 'Permit first the children to be satisfied, for it is not good to take the bread of the children and to throw it to the dogs' (7.27). The idea that God's gifts are for the Jews first, then subsequently for the Gentiles, lies at the heart of the theology of the Old Testament and of Judaism. Paul exemplifies this principle when he says that 'I am not ashamed of the gospel, for it is the power of God unto salvation to all who believe, to the Jew first and to the Greek' (Rom 1.16). The description of the Gentiles as dogs is also common. The use of the diminutive form ('little dogs') makes the slur no less offensive. Thus Jesus cites a proverb that reflects not only triumphalism, nationalism and ethnocentricity, but also uses a racial slur. What is the reader to do with such a statement? Is Jesus speaking tongue-in-cheek with a twinkle in his eye, knowing that both he and the woman have moved beyond such issues? Nothing in the story hints at this. Or is Jesus also a child of his own time, subject to inheriting stereotypes, narrow self-interest and racist language? While it is not sinful to inherit a limited world-view, it is sinful to retain and nourish it. It is not at all clear where Jesus begins in this scene; it is, however, clear where he ends up. The pejorative proverb from Jesus is answered in kind by the woman: 'Sir, even the dogs beneath the table are eating from the crumbs of the children' (7.28). Because of her answer, Jesus provides what she has requested—the healing of her daughter. Confirmation is provided upon her return to her home.

While this scene raises important questions about Christology—about who Jesus is—the story is concerned with a greater issue. Jesus has set out on a journey in which he proclaims and enacts the nearness of God's Reign. In doing so he crosses the various boundaries that separate humans from God—demons, sickness, stormy chaos, death, religious ritual. He also traverses the geographical boundary between Jew and Gentile territory. There he is confronted by a pushy foreign woman who demands that she, and her daughter, be included in the mercy of God. While it has been long understood that Gentiles are invited to come under God's care by embracing Jewish tradition, can a Gentile woman, standing on her own turf, invite herself into the circle of God's people? That is the social and religious boundary that remains, and this is precisely the line crossed in this story. The confrontation with the woman is not taken by Jesus as an affront, but as an occasion for dialogue and learning. The exchange between Jesus and this woman is typical of rabbinical instruction, and here the position of the woman wins out.

Surprising new insights are brought to the world of the story and thus to the reader. The borders of Israel have been crossed, figuratively and literally. The boundary separating Jew from Gentile has been breached. Proof of this is found in an insistent foreign woman who demands, and receives, the gift of God's healing.

Healing a Deaf and Silent Man (Mark 7.31-37)

Since Jesus has cast out demons, cleansed lepers, healed various illnesses and raised the dead, the healing of a man who cannot hear or speak should come as no surprise. The form of this story is rather typical: the miracle worker comes onto the scene; the need is presented; the victim is healed. From the perspective of this Gospel several new elements appear, but these too may be found in other miracle stories. The placing of the hands upon a victim is a common means of healing in such stories. The use of spit is also seen elsewhere. The use of a strange formula is common, though here the mystery is reduced when the narrator intrudes to translate the phrase. Likewise, the command to silence following the healing is known from similar stories. The absence of a conclusion ties this story to the scene that follows.

What is unusual about this story is its geographical and ideological setting. Geographically the scene occurs beside the lake in the region of Decapolis. This setting in Gentile territory will prove significant for this story and for the scenes that follow. Ideologically the language of the story invokes the world of the prophet Isaiah. The victim is described in 7.32 as deaf and 'hardly speaking'. This unusual description draws directly from the Septuagint (Greek) text of Isa. 35.6. The acclamation of 7.37—'he makes the deaf to hear and the unspeaking to speak'—reflects Isa. 35.5-10, where the opening of deaf ears and the loosing of silent tongues will accompany the regathering of Israel. For the reader who knows the Old Testament, the eschatological import of this connection is clear: in the ministry of Jesus the day of God's redemption has dawned, and it has done so in Decapolis among the Gentiles. Those who see this cannot be silenced; they begin to 'preach' and to acclaim the power of Jesus. Thus a rather typical healing story has been used to further define the work of Jesus and to demonstrate the power of the Kingdom to cross into uncharted realms.

Feeding Four Thousand (Mark 8.1-10)

It should come as no surprise that Jesus is able to feed the multitudes. The reader has already met such a story in Mk 6.32-46, where Jesus feeds a larger number of people (five thousand). What distinguishes this story from the earlier scene?

The internal elements that distinguish this story from Mk 6.32-46 are minor: differing numbers, blessings and baskets. These differences do not appear to hide deep symbolism.

A larger set of images are shared in common between the two feeding stories. The two stories share the same genre and form. The image of bread in the wilderness draws upon the exodus story. Dialogue occupies the centre of both stories. In both Jesus expresses compassion for the crowd. The disciples play a key role in both scenes. Thus Mk 8.1-10 is a mirror to the feeding story of Mk 6.32-46.

An alert reader may recognize that the major difference between these two stories is not what occurs or even how it occurs. The major difference between these scene is where they take place. Both stories take over the setting providing by their surrounding literary context. Mark 6.32-46 draws its geographical setting, which is Jewish, from the earlier stories (6.1, 6, 30-33). Internally, various images also point to a Jewish world-view: the exodus motif, the division of the crowd, the 12 baskets, the green grass (Ps. 23), the sheep/shepherd imagery. Mark 8.1-10 is set in a Gentile world. Jesus and his disciples have left Tyre, travelled through Sidon and entered the region of the Decapolis (7.31). Some also see the seven loaves (8.5) and seven baskets (8.8) as part of this contrast to the previous feeding.

These narrative techniques provide a dramatic sign for the reader: what Jesus has done among the Jewish people he now does among the Gentiles. Even as the healing of the Syro-Phoenician woman (7.24-31) and the deaf and silent man (7.31-37) extended Jesus' healing ministry to the Gentiles, so this story, through a gift miracle, extends the compassion of Jesus beyond the realm of Judaism. When the new exodus of God's people takes place, it will include both Jews and Gentiles.

As in the first feeding, the disciples play a key role in this story. It is they who raise question about the difficulties of the feeding (8.4), and it is they who distribute the food to the crowd (8.6-7). The story thus remains relevant in the world of the first reader, when followers of Jesus are confronted with the demands of their own time and their own people.

The character sketch of Jesus continues to grown in nuance and intensity. First through his healing and now through his blessing and feeding, Jesus has instigated a new movement—not unlike the exodus—among the people of God. In the process he has destroyed the boundary separating Jew and Gentile.

The Difficulty of Seeing (Mark 8.11-27a)

The wondrous power of Jesus has been openly displayed before his followers, before the crowds and even in the presence of religious authorities. In the Gospel of Mark these wondrous deeds demonstrate the authority of Jesus' teaching and proclaim the nearness of God's reign. This message has been taken through the villages of the Galilee, but also to Gentile territory.

Despite these demonstrations, faith and discipleship are not easily achieved in the Gospel of Mark. The third act of this Gospel (6.6b–8.27a) concludes with three scenes that demonstrate the barriers that remain.

In the first scene (8.11-13) Pharisees test Jesus with their request for a sign from heaven. The alert reader might remember that religious leaders have had ample opportunity to observe Jesus' wondrous deeds: the priest was sent the witness of a healed leper (1.44); the scribes observe the healing of a paralytic (2.1-12); Pharisees observe the healing of a man with a withered hand (3.1-6); Jesus heals the daughter of Jairus, the leader of a synagogue (5.21-24, 35-43). It should appear strange to the reader that religious authorities ask for another miracle from Jesus. The text is sensitive to this, for the term used here is not miracle or wonder, but 'sign'. In this account, religious leaders seek some heavenly demonstration given at the command of Jesus. The response of Jesus is dramatic, and his language is evocative: he groans in his spirit and replies with a Semitic phrase (similar to 1 Sam. 3.17) that is difficult to translate (literally: 'if a sign shall be given this generation…'). The phrase implies the speakers calling calamity upon themselves if the condition is ever fulfilled. The sense of the phrase is clear: this will not happen. Jesus thus rejects the quest for a certain faith, confirmed by signs from heaven. In the context of this Gospel the absurdity of the question is evident. The departure of Jesus to the other side is both geographical and ideological: all quests for certitude are abandoned. Within the larger story the irony of this request is inescapable: the Pharisees cannot see what is all about them.

The second scene (8.14-21) directs a similar frustration toward the disciples. The narrator notes that the disciples brought only one loaf for their boat trip (8.14). On the trip Jesus warns them of the leaven of the Pharisees and the Herodians. The symbolic language of Jesus is taken literally, leading to the discussion on the difficulties of discipleship. Here the disciples, who have also observed the ministry of Jesus, are described as hard-hearted, blind, deaf, forgetful. Jesus recalls in precise detail (8.19-20) the two feeding stories, which are full of symbolic meaning. Lack of bread is certainly not the issue here. This scene closes with a poignant question: 'Do you not yet understand?' (8.21). The disciples, and likely the reader, do not.

The third scene (8.22-27a) turns from dialogue to demonstration. This is a typical miracle unit, with its opening and closing movement (8.22, 27a), its presentation of the need, notice of the difficulty involved, a healing command, the giving of further instruction. The reader should not be surprised that Jesus can restore sight, since Jesus has healed various diseases in this Gospel and has even raised the dead. The difficult nature of the blindness becomes apparent when the healing requires two stages. The end result is satisfactory, however, for the sight is restored and the victim is sent home.

This difficult healing and the focus on seeing should alert the reader to a larger message. That Jesus can restore physical sight is certain, if difficult. Whether or not those around Jesus—religious leaders and disciples alike—will ever truly see who is he and what he is about is another question. He is surrounded by religious leaders who observe the dawning of the Kingdom, yet seek a sign. He is followed by disciples who do not understand, who do not see or hear or remember, who have not yet comprehended the way of discipleship. Thus the Gospel of Mark puts into narrative form the message conveyed in the parable of the sower (4.1-9). Despite the fertile nature of the Kingdom that Jesus proclaims, he is working in a tough field inhabited by obstinance, blindness and misunderstanding. The advent of the Kingdom in this place will require a miracle—a miracle even greater than the opening of blind eyes.

The Story Thus Far

The third act of this Gospel (6.6b-8.27a) is largely a repetition of the first two cycles (1.21-3.7a; 3.7-6.6). As in the previous acts Jesus gathers disciples, then travels throughout the land. Various accounts are given of Jesus' wondrous deeds and of his teaching ministry. Because familiar settings and typical forms are used to repeat a familiar pattern, the reader is invited to examine closely the details of these scenes for alterations, expansions, developments, reversals, surprises.

New details are added to the character sketch of Jesus in this act. In particular, his work is cast against the background of God's redemptive mission in the Old Testament. Even as Israel was guided by the leaders of the 12 tribes, so Jesus appoints 12 who will carry his work from village to village. Even as Moses provided bread in the wilderness, so Jesus feeds the hungry people, first with instruction, then with food. The appearance scene (6.47-53) surrounds Jesus with epiphanic images and plays upon the divine name. His interpretation and application of the law are demonstrated (7.1-23). Images from Isaiah suggest that the day of God's redemption has arrived (7.31-37). These connections to the Old Testament give sharper profile to the character of Jesus and to the nature of the Kingdom he is announcing.

Even more energy is given to the image of the disciples. They are given a new number (12), authority over unclean spirits (6.7), a new set of orders (6.8-11), a new name ('apostles' in 6.30). More importantly, their story and their destiny is linked with that of John and Jesus (6.7-31). New levels of expectation emerge: it is they who are responsible for the welfare of the crowds (6.32-46; 8.1-10). This new level of responsibility and expectation is accompanied by dramatic images of failure. The disciples do not wish to feed the crowds (6.35-36; 8.4); they think Jesus is a ghost on the sea at night (6.49) and are filled with terror (6.50). They do not understand what Jesus is saying (6.52; 8.16); they are blind and deaf and hardhearted and forgetful (8.17-18). Thus the irony of discipleship unfolds in this act.

In contrast to the rejection by religious leaders and the failure of disciples, a new line of characterization is emerging. While those expected to hear Jesus refuse to do so or struggle to understand, a positive response is found among those least expected to follow Jesus—a Syro-Phoenician woman, a deaf and silent man, a Gentile crowd. This unexpected line of characterization emerges precisely in correlation to the failure of others, giving the reader pause about the character map of the Kingdom.

Significant advances are also made in the plot line. The itinerant teaching ministry of Jesus in behalf of the Kingdom continues (6.6b). The ministry of Jesus is connected in new ways to the story of Israel. The power and presence of Yahweh are shown to be at work in the ministry of Jesus (6.47-53). Jesus' wondrous deeds continue (6.53-56). Important new boundaries are crossed in behalf of the Kingdom. The law is interpreted as a guide for humans rather than a ritual or legalistic code. The boundary excluding women and Gentiles from God's Kingdom is brought down. God's gathering of a new people is shown to include the crowds of Gentiles.

The singular boundary which resists all efforts is that of the human heart. Whether through obstinance or blindness, discipleship proves to be the most difficult miracle of all. These advances, and these difficulties, set the stage for the next act of Jesus' ministry.

Mark 8.27–10.52: From the Galilee to Jerusalem

The fourth act of this Gospel (8.27–10.52) moves beyond the pattern shared by the first three acts and serves as a bridge between the work in the Galilee and the final week in Jerusalem. The focus throughout is on the nature of discipleship and the difficulty of fulfilling this calling. At the same time important advances are made in the character sketch of Jesus. Particular attention is given to the growing threat surrounding his ministry. This act is also marked by a new pattern of movement, from Caesaraea Philippi to a high mountain, through the Galilee to Capernaum, to Judaea, to Jericho. At the end of the unit Jesus and his struggling disciples stand at the gates of Jerusalem, where the central themes of Christology, discipleship and suffering will be completed.

Of particular interest is the structuring of this act. Three passion predictions (8.31; 9.31; 10.32-34) provide the backbone of the unit. Each focuses on the identity of Jesus and the suffering that lies ahead. Each of the three is followed by instruction on discipleship, highlighting the continuing failure of the disciples. The fourth act is thus composed of three cycles of instruction. This fourth act is also framed by two positive images. The healing of a blind man precedes the act (8.22-26), and the healing of the blind Bartimaeus concludes the act (10.46-52). The reader is invited to connect these healing stories to the discipleship theme and to see that true discipleship is the greatest of all miracles.

Who Am I? (Mark 8.27-30)

The fourth act opens with two distinct changes in the story line: one is geographical and one is ideological. Notice is given of a new geographical direction (north beyond the Galilee to the headwaters of the Jordan in the region of Caesaraea Philippi). In the midst of this journey Jesus directly addresses, for the first time, the question of his identity.

The notice that he raises this issue 'in the way' (8.27) may already highlight the concern for discipleship. The sending of the Twelve in 6.7-13 is marked by instruction in what they should take 'for the way' (6.8). The term 'in the way' will become a clear image of discipleship in the story of Bartimaeus (10.52).

As they are in the way Jesus raises the pointed question of his identity. He first inquires of what others are saying. The answers (John the Baptist, Elijah, one of the prophets) all link Jesus to some aspect of Israel's history. The expectation of a prophet like Moses or the return of Elijah is fairly common in Jewish literature, and Herod is haunted by the prospect that John will return (Mk 6.16). These expectations also bear witness to the common belief that a dead servant of God can reappear or be raised from the dead. Neither Jesus nor the narrator comments on these opinions, leaving the reader to struggle with their role in the story and in the identity of Jesus.

Jesus then asks the disciples for their opinion on his identity. Peter provides the answer for the Twelve: you are the Christ. This clear, immediate response seems to indicate that Peter and the Twelve have finally embraced their calling, for this answer agrees with the opening line of the Gospel. What has been said by the narrator (1.1) and long understood by the reader seems to break at last upon the consciousness of the disciples. Thus it is strange and shocking that Jesus immediately silences this confession: they are to tell no one about him (8.30). This command becomes even more enigmatic when the reader recalls that the command to silence is a standard part of miracle stories, especially exorcisms. Departing demons are forbidden to make known the identity of Jesus (1.34). The confession of Peter is thus cast alongside the rantings of demons as inappropriate. The reader, ancient and modern, can only wonder at the meaning of this, for the content of the confession is correct: it has been stated at the beginning by a reliable narrator, and it will be confirmed at the end by Jesus himself (14.61-62). It is now clear that the disciples—and the reader—do not yet know what it means to name Jesus as the messiah of God. Thus Mk 8.27-30 opens this act by setting forth in dramatic tones the misunderstanding that surrounds the destiny and the identity of Jesus. While they know the right words, the disciples—and the reader—need to be taught more. That is precisely the goal of the units which follow.

The Suffering Son of Man (Mark 8.31-33)

The pronouncement in this story casts the identity of Jesus in new dimensions. The components for this scene are drawn for the previous story line, but they are assembled here in a new way with stark clarity. Moving away from the Christ confession of the previous scene, the son of man title is employed to speak of Jesus' earthly destiny. In contrast to the power associated with his words and deeds, Jesus' future is marked by suffering. The controversy with religious leaders developed in earlier scenes will soon turn deadly. Jesus thus opens for the disciples a new chapter in his identity: he is the son of man who will suffer and die at the hands of religious leaders. One further stroke is added to the portrait: he who raised the dead will himself be raised.

Picking up on earlier themes, this pronouncement from Jesus is described as 'teaching' (8.31). Previously Jesus' teaching centred on the Kingdom of God, it was marked by authority and it was demonstrated in the wonders he performed. Now the teaching of Jesus centres on the suffering of the one they have named as messiah. Previously the 'word' was an image for the Gospel (eight times in Mk 4.14-20); here the word points to the bad news of Jesus' suffering and death.

The idea of a suffering messiah, which is difficult to demonstrate in pre-Christian Judaism, would appear to the first reader as a contradiction in terms (something like a cowardly hero or a wise fool). Peter gives voice to this objection. The dramatic language used to convey the exchange between Peter and Jesus is taken from the exorcism stories. Peter rebukes Jesus and Jesus rebukes him back. Peter is cast in the image of Satan, and his thinking is declared to be guided by human concerns.

Thus this short scene sets in place the major work for the fourth act of the Gospel. The disciples are no better off than the demons and do not rise above common human perception in their understanding of Jesus. The most difficult boundary has not yet been crossed. Their identification of Jesus as the messiah is flawed and must be commanded to silence, for they are not yet willing to embrace his destiny of suffering and death. Though they have been taught by Jesus, they have much to learn about who he is and what it means to follow him. The reader who has followed their cues also has much to learn. To this task the remaining scenes of this act are devoted.

Real Discipleship (Mark 8.34-9.1)

Following the failure of Peter to grasp the stark teaching on death, Jesus turns to the crowds, with the disciples included. He describes the true traits of discipleship: following after Jesus requires self-denial, taking up one's cross, losing one's soul for the sake of Jesus and the gospel, being unashamed of Jesus and his words. The portrait of discipleship has been sketched in stark new tones of suffering and service. The cross does not serve here as a symbol of Jesus' death, and none of the three passion predictions mention the cross. The cross is instead a symbol of discipleship in the path of Jesus. The soul of which Jesus speaks is, in Hebrew thought, the self and not a spiritual dimension contrasted to the physical. Here the contrast to the soul is the world. Thus discipleship is framed in an earthly context as suffering and service after the model of

Jesus. This earthly frame has a future dimension, however. What one decides about the life and words of Jesus in this age determines the verdict by the son of man in the age to come. The continuity between present and future is reinforced by the prediction of 9.1: some who follow Jesus in this age will be present when the Kingdom of God comes in power. Almost as an afterthought the Kingdom has received a futuristic dimension, and this has been attached to the figure of the coming son of man. Thus the task of following Jesus, which was previously set along the Lake of Galilee (1.16-20; 5.1-20) and in the villages of the Galilee (6.7-13, 30-31), has been transposed into a larger dimension and pointed specifically toward self-sacrifice. This is the calling that the disciples do not yet grasp.

The True Nature of Jesus (Mark 9.2-10)

Even as 8.34-9.1 sets discipleship in a next dimension, so the scene in 9.2-10 modulates the question of Jesus' identity to a new level. Through its setting the scene is prepared as a moment of revelation. The first reader may remember that Moses spent six days on Sinai in preparation for God's revelation. The first reader knows that mountains are a place of revelation in Jewish stories. The appearance of Moses and Elijah to converse with Jesus places him in the company of Israel's primal lawgiver and Israel's paradigmatic prophet. The white clothing of Jesus confirms this otherworldly scene. Something new is being said about Jesus. His work in behalf of God's Kingdom is not limited to the earthly scenes of his ministry; he has a greater role in Israel's history that places him alongside Moses and Elijah. Through this scene the Christology of the Gospel of Mark—its characterization of Jesus—is taken to its highest level.

Alongside this new revelation, which is observed by Peter, James and John, stands a stark reminder of the failure of the disciples. Having seen this transformation of Jesus, Peter addresses him by an earthly title— rabbi. Peter wishes to stay on the mountain and to build shrines there. The narrator confirms the inappropriateness of Peter's response: he does not know what to say. All of the disciples are filled with fear. Such fear is normal in the face of an epiphany, but the reader has learned to associate the fear of the disciples with misunderstanding and cowardice (Mk 4.40-41).

The final lines of this scene unite the earthly portrait of Jesus with this revelation. As in the Old Testament, the presence of God takes the form of a cloud. The voice from the cloud declares both the identity of Jesus (this is my beloved son) and the demand for discipleship (hear him). The first reader knows that this Hebraic term calls for obedience. At the end of the story only Jesus remains with the disciples.

Those who read this text and seek to follow Jesus are left with new insights and haunting images. The Jesus who calls disciples to follow him in the Galilee belongs to the ages, yet his closest followers have not yet understood. They will be offered no further visions and no tangible evidence of this experience, but only the presence of Jesus, the haunting questions he evokes and the continuing call to discipleship.

The descent scene (9.9-10) gives further context to the transfiguration. The disciples are again commanded to silence. This scene will make sense only when the son of man has been raised from the dead. Though they have heard the prediction of Jesus' death, suffering and resurrection, they do not understand (9.10). Thus this larger scene (9.2-10) offers at once clarification and confusion.

Further Instruction on the Death of the Son of Man (Mark 9.11-13)

The need for more instruction leads to a question from the disciples: why do the scribes say that Elijah must come first (9.11)? Jesus accepts this prediction from Malachi that Elijah will come and restore all things before the day of Yahweh (Mal. 4.5-6). Jesus declares that Elijah indeed has already come, they did to him what they wished and the Scripture is fulfilled. Jesus thus declares that John the Baptist was Elijah and that the way now stands open for the day of Yahweh. Jesus' answer exceeds their question: not only the suffering of the Baptist is to be seen in the Scriptures, but also the suffering of the son of man (9.12).

These enigmatic sayings define a new line for Israel's history. Elijah has come in the form of John the Baptist, suffering and preparing for the day of Yahweh. Jesus' ministry, which will be marked by suffering and death, is the story of the son of man to whom the future belongs. These new claims about Jesus are placed before the wondering disciples, but also before the reader of the Gospel.

Failure to Heal; Failure to Believe (Mark 9.14-29)

Surprisingly, a miracle story completes the first cycle of instruction in the fourth act. Since the miracles of Jesus reached a climax in the mass exorcism in Gadara (5.1-20) and in the raising of the daughter of Jairus (5.21-43), this scene has another point. Emphasis is given to the difficulty of the healing. This typical motif found in other miracle stories is highlighted here in order to address the dangers of discipleship.

With the entrance of Jesus, the description of the illness and the request for healing, the stage is set for a typical exorcism story. What is distinct here is the inability of the disciples to cast out the demon, especially in light of their previous success (6.12-13). This impotence is amplified in the response of Jesus: describing this generation as unbelieving, he asks how long he must endure them (9.19). The difficulty of the healing is confirmed in typical fashion when the demon acts out in the presence of Jesus (9.20). In a strange twist Jesus calmly discusses the disease with the father while the child is rolling about in seizures, foaming at the mouth (9.21-22). The focus on the difficulty of the healing moves away from the suffering child to the question of the faith of the father (9.22-24). The healing occurs through a command from Jesus as the crowd approaches. The difficulty is conveyed in the deathlike appearance of the child, and a second healing act occurs in the raising up of the child.

Failure is emphasized in the closing verses when the disciples inquire about their inability to heal. Only prayer can do this, says Jesus, suggesting not only the traditional motif of the difficulty of the cure, but also suggesting another area of deficiency among the disciples—failure to pray properly.

Thus a rather typical story form has been intensified and focused on the issue of faith. In contrast to the successful healing by Jesus stands the impotence of the disciples and the wavering faith of the father. The reader should recognize in this failure and in the frustration of Jesus that the disciples have regressed beyond the level of the initial cycles of ministry. In the matter of comprehension, prayer, faith and courage, the disciples have far to go.

The Suffering Son of Man, Once Again (Mark 9.30-32)

The cycle of announcement, failure and teaching is repeated in the scenes that follow. In Mk 9.30-32 Jesus seeks to be alone with his disciples in order to teach them. The christological revelation of 8.31 is repeated: the son of man will be handed over to death, but he will be raised three days later. As in 8.31-33 the description of Jesus' identity and destiny is not grasped by the disciples: they do not understand this saying, and they are afraid to ask questions (9.32).

Failure to Understand, Again (Mark 9.33-37)

The failure of the disciples reaches a low point in the scene that follows the second passion prediction. When they come into Capernaum Jesus asks about a conversation the disciples had 'in the way'. They are silent, for they do not wish to admit that they were arguing over which of them is the greatest. This failure is followed by a new attempt to teach on discipleship. Jesus 'calls' the Twelve, perhaps hinting at starting over. As in the previous cycle (8.34–9.1), the theme of service and self-sacrifice is emphasized. In a proverbial saying those who wish to be first are called to be last of all and servant (deacon) of all. This term was previously used to refer to the household service rendered by Peter's mother-in-law (1.31).

Jesus then teaches through example, placing a child before them. His message links service to Christology. To receive a child in the name of Jesus is to receive Jesus; to receive Jesus is to receive the one who sent him. Thus one's entrance into God's Kingdom and one's obedience to Jesus is shown not in one's claim to greatness, but in the humility and compassion that serves even the children.

Real Discipleship, Once Again (Mark 9.38-40)

The failed viewpoint of the disciples is exposed further in their attempt to stop a person, not from their group, who is ministering in Jesus' name. Jesus turns from the narrow question of inclusion to one of practice and applies the most liberal of standards for discipleship: one not against us is for us.

Instructions for Disciples (Mark 9.41-50)

Turning from the ideology of discipleship—last of all, servant of all, like a child, with us—Jesus addresses the practice of discipleship. What follows is a collection of proverbs and sayings with little logical connection. Their thematic unity is their focus on the deeds of discipleship. Their formal unity is established through catchword connections which lead from one saying to another. This pattern can be seen around several terms:

1. The 'little ones' of 9.42 picks up the 'child' of 9.36;
2. The name of Jesus connects 9.41 to 9.38 and 9.39;
3. A series of sayings flows from the 'scandalized' theme: 9.42, 43, 45, 47;
4. The image of fire connects a series of sayings: 9.44, 48, 49;
5. The related image of Gehenna connects several sayings: 9.44, 45, 47;
6. The image of salt is found five times in 9.49-50.

These catchword connections suggest that this material comes from an oral collection based on form more than content. While some sayings prove enigmatic ('for all shall be salted with fire') and the logical connections are obscure, this miscellaneous collection of teaching material serves in the Gospel of Mark as instruction on discipleship.

Instruction on Marriage (Mark 10.1-12)

Since this segment of the story line has become the focal point for Jesus' teaching material, further examples are added to the loose collection. Mk 10.1-12 deals with the issue of marriage and adultery. This unit is separated from the previous scene by the note of transition (10.1) and the change in audience (10.2). This unit of teaching material is addressed to the crowds, and it is presented as typical of Jesus' work.

In connection with this general notice a debate scene occurs (10.3-9), followed by private instruction to the disciples (10.10-12). In this controversy the Pharisaic dependence on the law of Moses is supplanted by Jesus' concern for the will of God. Behind the concessions of Moses, Jesus claims, the intent of God remains valid: marriages are intended as enduring unions.

In the Gospel of Mark 'the house' becomes a place of private instruction in discipleship. Therefore Jesus gives more specific interpretation of marriage law to his disciples in the privacy of the house (10.10-12). The egalitarian nature of this rule is as surprising as its starkness: to divorce and to remarry is adultery (10.11-12).

Children and the Kingdom (Mark 10.13-16)

Further teaching occurs in Mk 10.13-16, but the theme of discipleship failure reappears in connection with this instruction. In addition the central focus on the Kingdom re-emerges.

Someone brings a child to Jesus, and three positive elements follow. First, the child is embraced and blessed by Jesus. Secondly, the child is shown to be indicative of the Kingdom. Finally, the child provides a model for entering the Kingdom.

In contrast to the positive elements spawned by the visit of the child, one negative theme is developed. Even as the disciples forbid the actions of outsiders in the name of Jesus (9.38-40), so they rebuke those who bring the child to Jesus (10.13). A linguistic tie connects the two scenes: in both Jesus responds to the disciples' defensiveness with the command 'do not hinder him/them' (9.39; 10.14). The reader is thus directed to envision a wider frame for discipleship.

Wealth and the Kingdom (Mark 10.17-31)

The teaching unit that follows also presents instruction that could fit into a number of contexts. At the same time important themes from the larger story are highlighted.

To the alert reader the scene offers the prospect of a new beginning on the road of discipleship. The initial movement (10.17) signals a new event. The setting 'in the way' suggests a discipleship motif. The running and bowing before Jesus recall from other scenes the eagerness to get near Jesus. The address of Jesus as Teacher, the serious theological question, the discussion over Scripture, Jesus' love for the questioner and the mention of 'the word' all paint the scene with images of calling and discipleship. The interaction with Scripture and the claim to have observed the commandments suggests this is a Jewish person who comes to Jesus seeking the way of God. Perhaps someone will at last get it right. But this one also fails the test. The questioner will not give up the one thing that prevents faithful following of Jesus—wealth. The questioner will not cross this final boundary separating him from eternal life.

A careful reader may notice that the language has shifted from the role of the Kingdom to the place of heaven and eternal life. This may signal that the primary audience is no longer the people of Jesus' day, who heard him speak of the nearness of the Kingdom, but a later audience that now frames the question in terms of heaven and eternal life.

This teaching scene, which may be applied to a variety of contexts and audiences, is followed by a scene of private instruction. Here the question of the faithfulness of Jesus' disciples re-emerges. This scene returns to traditional forms (pronouncement, simile, hyperbole) and to traditional themes (the Kingdom).

Following the stark pronouncement that it is difficult for the rich to enter the Kingdom, the disciples object, signalling once again their resistance to Jesus' message of sacrifice and suffering. Jesus repeats the pronouncement through hyperbole and simile: a rich person entering heaven is like a camel passing through the eye of a needle. The intensification of the pronouncement is met by intensification of the objection by the disciples. Their world-view is unveiled in their question: if the rich cannot be saved, who can? The answer by Jesus places the whole scene in theological perspective: none can, except by the grace of God.

The close of the scene again unveils the self-interest of the disciples. If suffering and sacrifice are the key, then Peter declares that they have left everything to follow Jesus. The answer of Jesus takes up this line of reasoning, but with key alterations. The disciples will receive back what they gave up—and more. A part of the 'more' is persecution (10.30). Following the context of the larger unit, their reward will be for this age, but also life eternal in the age to come.

Even this straightforward logic ends with a twist. Many who are first will be last, and many last will be first. Thus discipleship cannot be measured out upon a scale of sacrifice and reward.

The alert reader may recognize that the whole unit is a loose collection of teaching material that has minimal connections to a central theme. The reader may also recognize a recurring play upon the parable of the sower (4.3-9). The wealthy questioner is grieved at 'the word' and goes away. Jesus' lesson on the camel declares that those with riches will find it hard to enter the Kingdom, and the disciples are amazed at 'his words' (10.24). Jesus says that those who have left fields behind will receive fields back (10.29, 30). As the parable of the sower predicts, they will be rewarded a hundredfold (4.8; 10.30).

The need of the disciples for further instruction (9.33-37) provides the occasion for this Gospel to gather a wide variety of teaching material into this act. The theme of this collected material is only loosely related to the immediate concerns of this act, and the audience is not limited to the first telling of the story.

The Suffering Son of Man, a Third Time (Mark 10.32-34)

The suffering and death of Jesus is again predicted, initiating the third cycle of prediction–failure–instruction. As in other trilogies in the Gospel of Mark, a pattern of development can be seen. The third prediction is the most complex and revealing of the three. First, the setting is more precise and more dramatic. The disciples go with Jesus 'in the way', and they are headed for Jerusalem. Jesus is described as 'going before them' (10.32), and this term will be picked up in the promise of Mk 16.7. Secondly, the failure of the disciples is built into the prediction: they are amazed and they follow with fear (10.32). This fear will also be picked up at the close of the Gospel (16.8). Thirdly, the destination in Jerusalem is specified for the first time. Fourthly, the handing over to the Gentiles is first predicted. Fifthly, new images of abuse are introduced: condemned, mocked, spit upon, scourged. This third passion prediction stands as a climactic pronouncement not only because it completes the trilogy, but also because it gives the fullest account of Jesus' suffering and death.

Failure to Understand, Again (Mark 10.35-45)

Even as the third prediction provides the starkest prophecy of Jesus' death, so the third account of failure is the most dramatic. In the aftermath of the stark prophecy of Jesus' death, the sons of Zebedee ask that Jesus give them what they desire. They seek to sit at Jesus' right and his left when he comes into his glory. This self-serving request is a rejection of all that Jesus has taught on service, suffering, being last. The address of Jesus as Teacher highlights this irony. The phrase 'you do not know what you are asking' recalls the response of Peter at the transfiguration

(9.6). Jesus then points to his own suffering and death, using the images of a cup and a baptism, and he asks if the disciples are able to share this along with his glory. Their brash answer—'We are able'—recalls their impotence over the demon in 9.28—'Why were we not able to cast it out?' Jesus leaves the question of who will sit at his left and right unanswered, but he does offer a prophecy about the future of the disciples: they will suffer with him.

The failure of John and James spreads to the rest of the Twelve (10.41), who are indignant at the request of the sons of Zebedee. Jesus responds to this failure by offering further instruction in discipleship. Jesus 'calls' the disciples once again (10.42), then offers the true standard for discipleship: greatness is found in service. This standard is modelled in the activity of Jesus himself and leads to a new understanding of his identity: he is the son of man who will serve and will give his life in exchange for the people (10.45). This final saying unites the two central themes of this Gospel: who Jesus is and what it means to follow him.

The Miracle of Discipleship (Mark 10.46-52)

The threefold pattern of passion prediction–failure–instruction concludes with a miracle story. Since the healing of a blind person has already been demonstrated (8.22-26) and this earlier story is more dramatic, the purpose of Mk 10.46-52 is not found in its content, but in its context. That Jesus can open blind eyes is no new message; that he does so in the context of the disciples' failure creates an ironic contrast to their blindness. This emphasis is highlighted by the use of two stories of restoring sight (8.22-26; 10.46-52) to frame this section on the blindness of the disciples.

In addition to the location of this miracle, various aspects of this scene point to the issue of discipleship. The note that Bartimaeus sits 'beside the way' suggests that a discipleship motif is at work. The confession of Jesus as 'Son of David' strengthens this image. 'He calls you' they tell Bartimaeus, and the alert reader knows this term has been used for the calling of disciples. Other aspects strengthen the discipleship motif: Bartimaeus addresses Jesus as 'rabboni', a Hebrew word for teacher; Jesus declares that the faith of Bartimaeus has healed him; after the healing Bartimaeus 'follows' Jesus—another term for discipleship. For the alert reader the discipleship of Bartimaeus is made certain in the closing line: 'And immediately he saw again, and he begins to follow him in the way.' In contrast to the self-interest and obstinacy of the Twelve, the ideal for discipleship has been demonstrated in a blind beggar from Jericho.

For the alert reader, one final connection establishes the contrast between the Twelve and Bartimaeus. Jesus asks of Bartimaeus the same question he asked of the James and John: What do you want me to do for you? (10.36, 51). James and John ask for positions of power and glory, leading to conflict among their companions. Bartimaeus asks for sight and uses it to follow Jesus 'in the way'. That way will lead to Jerusalem.

The Story Thus Far

The fourth act of this Gospel (8.27-10.52) stands in contrast to the first three acts (1.21-3.7a; 3.7-6.6; 6.6b-8.27a). The first three acts were framed around a common pattern: a notice of Jesus' ministry (1.14-15; 3.7-12; 6.6b), a call to disciples (1.16-20; 3.13-19; 6.7-13), teaching and healing in various scenes, a closing scene of rejection (3.1-6; 6.1-6; 8.14-21). The fourth act moves forward from this pattern to create its own cycles. Framed around three passion predictions (8.31; 9.31; 10.32-34), the fourth act builds three cycles of prediction–failure–instruction. This structural design has a profound impact upon the dynamics of this unit.

The settings of this act do not change often, and the geographical locations rarely impact the story. With fewer transitions, this act takes on a more stable ethos. Three types of setting do take on greater significance in this act. The mountain becomes a clear place of revelation (9.2-8). The 'way' becomes a clear image for discipleship. The house becomes a place of private instruction. Thus the settings of Mk 8.27-10.52 are more ideological than geographical, and the focus of each is instruction.

A similar pause can be observed in the plot line. Little real action occurs in this unit. Apart from the two miracle stories (9.14-29; 10.46-52), the remainder of the unit is given over to instruction.

The static nature of this act is also seen in the use of genres. While the first three acts employs various standard types—miracle stories, pronouncement scenes, controversy scenes, parables—this act makes little use of such types. Even the teaching material is loosely organized, with no particular form dominating. The teaching focus attracts to itself a large collection of didactic material.

Despite the static nature of setting and plot, this unit makes important advances in characterization. A new understanding of Jesus is reached: he is the son of man who will suffer and serve, but also the son of man who will come in glory. He will die in Jerusalem in behalf of the people.

Similar strides are made in the characterization of the disciples, but in a negative direction. While they have struggled throughout, they are characterized here by blindness, self-concern, misperception, failure. An inverse relation has been created: the more precisely the character of

Jesus is revealed to the disciples, the greater their failure to understand
and to follow him.

In subtle ways this act also brings new information to the reader.
While the teaching of Jesus previously focused on the Kingdom of God
and the demonstration of Jesus' authority, little attention was given to
content. In contrast this unit offers detailed information on what Jesus
taught. As in previous acts the teaching of Jesus is connected to the
Kingdom and to the 'word', but new connections are also established:
eternal life, heaven, salvation, the coming of the son of man, the suffering of the son of man.

Despite these new contributions, the central focus on characterization
remains. Through the triad that dominates the unit Jesus is revealed as
the son of man who will suffer and die in Jerusalem, then reign in glory.
The disciples are shown to be impotent, unable to understand, unwilling
to follow. Only in the model of Bartimaeus do we find a glimmer of
hope. True discipleship, like true sight, is a miraculous gift. For those
closest to Jesus this is the greatest boundary of all, and it has not yet
been crossed.

Mark 11.1-13.37: Ministry in Jerusalem

The conflict between Jesus and the religious leadership will dominate the fifth act of this Gospel (11.1-13.37). This conflict was prominent in Mark 1-3, but almost absent from Mark 4-10. In the first act (1.21-3.7a) the authority of Jesus' teaching is demonstrated in miracle stories, and these scenes lead to conflict with some of the religious leaders. The fifth act will reintroduce this tension as the background for the story of Jesus' suffering and death in Jerusalem. As in 2.1-3.6 the tension here between Jesus and the religious leaders culminates in a death plot. Mk 11.1-13.37 employs a host of literary forms and strategies to narrate this conflict.

Entering Jerusalem (Mark 11.1-11)

The story of Jesus is set within the heart of Judaism. He has dealt with various components of Jewish piety: synagogue, Scripture, prayer, fasting, alms, messianic expectations, purity laws. Ironically Jesus has not visited Jerusalem, and the temple has played no role in the story up to this point. In Mk 11.1-11 Jesus comes at last to Jerusalem and to the temple.

This scene is set against a backdrop of Old Testament imagery and piety. The entrance into Jerusalem echoes the scene from Zech. 9.9, where Israel's king enters amid shouting, riding on a donkey. The spreading of garments before Jesus recalls the coronation of King Jehu in 2 Kgs 9.13. The blessing shouted by the crowd contains echoes of various Old Testament passages (Pss. 118.25; 148.1; Job 16.19). The reader will recognize in this scene and in upcoming scenes that the Jewish context of the story emerges most clearly within the confines of Jerusalem. This scene carries within it the joy and hope and pride of Israel: Jesus is declared a king in the line of David and welcomed into David's city.

Yet this scene also carries signs of the conflict and tragedy about to unfold. The first viewpoint of Jesus is from the Mount of Olives (11.1) and the city of Jerusalem is 'opposite them' (11.2). This symbolic geography will be developed as a sign of tension in subsequent scenes. When Jesus arrives, at last, at the temple, he 'looks about' at everything (11.11)—a gesture that elsewhere in the Gospel indicates hostility (3.5, 34; 5.32; 10.23). A temporal sign is also used to hint at what is to come: when Jesus comes to the temple, 'the hour is late' and he departs. Thus the reader who has been alerted by the earlier scenes of conflict and has listened to the passion predictions may already find, amid the pilgrim's welcome into Jerusalem, a shadow of things to come.

The Curse (Mark 11.12-25)

The opening scene in Jerusalem recalls numerous motifs from the Galilean ministry: Jesus uses an object from nature to teach, he performs a miracle, he 'casts out' (11.15), the people are astonished at his teaching, his teaching results in conflict. Still the story is tailored to its setting. In the temple he quotes the Scripture about God's house. His opponents are the chief priests and the scribes. Jesus is addressed by his followers as rabbi, the Jewish term for teacher (11.21). Here, in the sight of the temple, he gives his longest teaching on prayer. Thus the story of Jesus established in the Galilee is being re-established in Jerusalem with particular reference to the temple.

This scene returns, for the final time, to the literary form that dominates this Gospel: the miracle story. The first three acts developed the miracle story into a complex literary tool and demonstrated the most dramatic forms of miracles (raising the dead, calming the lake, a mass exorcism). These earlier miracles were each about liberation: crossing a boundary that separates people from God's Reign. Why repeat another miracle story in this context, and why tell one that appears to be so self-serving? The alert reader will recognize that this story is not significant so much for its content or its outcome as it is for the literary and theological connections it establishes.

The events of the miracle story (11.12-14; 20-26) are rather straightforward, though they are enigmatic. The story is built around two cycles of movement: they go out from Bethany on the second day (11.12), then they take the same route on the morning of the third day (11.20). In this story the typical miracle form is stretched in extraordinary ways. The movement of Jesus presents the need. There is no victim, only the hunger of Jesus. There is no healing command, only a curse. The results are not immediate, though they are dramatic. There is a recognition and acclamation of the miracle, but nothing positive results. No one is liberated, but a tree is killed.

We have here an enigmatic caricature of a miracle story. While other miracles contributed to the character of Jesus, this one calls it into question. Who is this that speaks to trees, demanding they serve him, then curses them and kills them? As it is intended to do, the story creates chaos and confusion and dislocation for one who has read the rest of this story. And that is the point. This scene is not about fig trees. Lest a clumsy reader miss this, the narrator offers a rare intrusion to complete the collapse of the scene. Jesus demands fruit from the tree, but, says the narrator, it was not the season for figs (11.13).

The reader who seeks the significance of this event is forced to look beyond the bounds of the miracle story. But the reader does not have to look far. The story of the fig tree has been broken open and another scene has been inserted. The reader experienced in the ways of this Gospel will recognize here an interpolation—a story within a story. From previous experience the reader will know that this literary technique shapes the telling of the stories, but also that each story becomes the frame for interpreting the other. So it is with these scenes.

The inner story (11.15-19) has its own coherence, and it could stand alone. The story opens and closes with movement (11.15, 19), forming the boundaries of the unit. This is a scene of action, and the words from Jesus are taken mostly from Scripture. The reader who grasps the setting of the story will understand its dramatic impact. At the season of the Jewish Passover, when Jerusalem is filled with nationalistic passion and overrun by Roman troops, Jesus creates havoc in the temple. Neither the leaders of Israel nor those of Rome will tolerate such actions, and the stage is set for the events which follow.

Apart from the dramatic action of this scene, a distinct portrait of the temple is offered to the reader. Jesus finds the temple filled with people who are buying and selling, people who are changing money, people who are selling pigeons for sacrifice. He finds others who are taking vessels through the temple, apparently using the place of worship as a shortcut.

The actions of Jesus are surprising in the context of this Gospel. His previous actions are limited to a few, very docile images: he travels from place to place, he places his hands on the sick, he confronts demons and storms with words alone, he teaches. Nowhere else in this Gospel is the zeal of Jesus demonstrated in such deeds. Here he overturns tables, drives out vendors, prevents the thoroughfare.

This scene proves important for the plotting of this Gospel, for the events in the temple initiate a death plot (11.18) and may provide the grounds for incrimination (14.58). In addition this scene adds an important element to the characterization of Jesus. Upon the first reading Jesus' actions may seem to set him over against the faith and heritage of Israel. The first readers would likely recognize that Jesus is quoting from the Old Testament prophets (Isa. 56.7; Jer. 7.11). Isaiah and Jeremiah both condemned Israel's worship in the temple, and they did so in the name of Yahweh. This scene casts Jesus in the image of the faithful prophet who calls Israel back to the worship of God by condemning the temple.

The closing lines of the temple scene pick up the heart of the Galilean ministry and cast it into the Jerusalem context. As in the Galilee (1.22) the people here are amazed at the teaching of Jesus, which centres more on deeds than on words (11.18). As in the Galilee (3.6) religious leaders here observe the deeds of Jesus and plot his death (11.18).

The closing line of the temple scene demonstrates the power of the narrative to speak at multiple levels. At the end of the day Jesus goes home. Yet the alert reader sees more. The end of the temple has come, and the followers of Jesus move on. For those readers living in the aftermath of the first Jewish war (66-74 CE), Jesus has prophesied the events they have experienced.

Thus the reader is invited to taste the enigma of the fig tree (11.12-14), then to observe the temple events (11.15-19), then to understand the connection between the two (11.20-25). The first reader may also know that the fig tree is a symbol for Israel in the Old Testament (Isa. 34.4; Jer. 8.13; 29.17; Hos. 2.12; 9.10, 16; Joel 1.7; Mic. 7.1-6). In Isa. 34.4 and Hos. 2.12 the destruction of the fig tree is a sign of God's judgment. The connection between the fig tree and the temple proves crucial to the narration of this Gospel. The events of Mk 11.12-25 instigate the plot line that will control the remainder of this story. The central component of Jesus' character is also put into place: he is the prophet from God whose teaching to Israel will lead to his death. All of these components are framed for the new setting in Jerusalem.

The final section of the unit (11.22-25) provides private instruction to the disciples. The advice given here is related to the immediate context, but it also speaks to the concerns of the first reader. Strangely the focus turns from the enigma of the fig tree and the drama of the temple to the question of faith and prayer. How can this dramatic scene be transported into the world of the first reader, who lives in the aftermath of the fall of Jerusalem, or into the world of later readers? The key is to be found in faith in God. Disciples are asked to believe that they can cast mountains into the sea. Since not even Jesus has done this, how should the disciple proceed? Once again the reader is nudged to look beyond the literal. The mountain is not any mountain, but 'this mountain' (11.23). One mountain (or hill) visible to the disciples is the Mount of Olives, which plays a prominent role in the last acts of this Gospel (11.1; 13.3; perhaps in 14.32). Some readers may find here a reference to Zech. 14.1-5, where Jerusalem will be destroyed and the Mount of Olives split into two pieces before Yahweh comes to restore all things. Is this the prayer the reader is to pray, particularly in the aftermath of the fall of Jerusalem in the 70s? Other readers may take clues from the text itself and point to the other mountain visible to the disciples—the temple mount. The first reader in the 70s knows that Jerusalem has fallen and the temple has been destroyed. Jesus himself will predict this (13.2), and he will do so 'sitting upon the Mount of Olives over against the temple' (13.3). The first reader is invited to find here a prophecy of the things that have occurred, as well as instruction in how to move forward. Guided by faith in God, the believer can move on from the fall of Jerusalem to a life of prayer and forgiveness. Thus the temple piety is replaced with the central piety of the Old Testament: love God and love your neighbour (Deut. 6.4-5; Lev. 19.18). This demand will be repeated in the teaching of Jesus in the temple (Mk 12.32-34). The fallen temple will be replaced by an authentic piety drawn from God's covenant with Israel. The story has offered its first hints that even the death of Jesus and the subsequent destruction of the temple may be overcome. The readers of this Gospel are thus invited to listen over the shoulders of the disciples and to hear the teaching of Jesus for their own age.

The Gospel of Mark thus reveals itself to be a complex piece of literature entirely conscious of its use of images, signs, structures to guide the reader through the story of Jesus. In a variation upon the miracle story form, the tale of the fig tree has been deconstructed in order to connect it to the story of the temple. This strategy creates a sign that foreshadows the remaining events of the story and interprets the world of the first reader.

Teaching in the Temple (Mark 11.27-12.44)

The conflict with the temple has been demonstrated in dramatic form in a scene reminiscent of the Old Testament prophets (Mk 11.12-25). The scenes that follow demonstrate this conflict through Jesus' own teaching, and these scenes are also set in the temple (11.27; 12.35). A clear formal pattern is established for this instruction and conflict: religious figures parade one after another before Jesus to question him. In succession come the chief priests, scribes, elders (11.27-33); the Pharisees and Herodians (12.13-17); the Sadduccees (12.18-27); the scribes (12.28-40); then finally the disciples (13.1-2). The question of 11.28 poses the central focus of this string of debates: 'In what authority are you doing these things?'

Chief Priests, Scribes, Elders (11.27-33)

The first debate is linked cleanly to the drama in the temple. That scene ends with a death plot by the chief priests and the scribes and with the notice that they fear Jesus because of the crowd (11.18). This information is taken into the first debate, where chief priests, scribes and now elders refuse to answer Jesus because they fear the crowd (11.32). Little new information is given in the first debate, since Jesus and the leaders refuse to answer each other's question. What is demonstrated here is the rhetorical agility of Jesus. In addition this debate recalls the connection between the ministry of John and that of Jesus, stirring again the prophetic overtones of his character sketch.

Pharisees and Herodians (12.13-17)
The second debate scene represents an attempt by the Pharisees and Herodians to trap Jesus in his teaching (12.13). After an opening compliment the Pharisees ask a question with no good answer: should we pay taxes to the Romans? The rhetorical skill of Jesus emerges again when he splits the question. The coin that they bring to Jesus bears the image and the inscription of Caesar. It is his, says Jesus, so give it back to him. Implied in the answer is that humans, who bear God's image, belong to God. The first reader would likely know that this answer is acceptable to both Roman and Jew. Romans could care less about religious values if taxes are paid and the peace is kept. In a strict Jewish world-view the coin of Caesar is unclean and bears an idolatrous image: one should not take it, much less keep it. At the end of this debate the religious leaders, like so many crowds before, are amazed at the teaching of Jesus.

Sadduccees (12.18-27)
The Sadduccees take their turn, bringing to Jesus a question most likely aimed at the Pharisees and their belief in a resurrection from the dead. Citing the Mosaic law of levirate marriage, the Sadduccees create a twisted legal case designed to ridicule the conception of an afterlife. Since the Sadduccees employed Scripture to pose the question, Jesus counters with Scripture. There is no right answer for the wrong question, Jesus implies, then levels a more personal rebuttal: you do not know the Scripture nor the power of God (12.24). Jesus' understanding of Scripture in these passages draws heavily upon Jewish writings found in the book of Enoch.

Jesus then takes the question to a new level, demonstrating his agility with the Scriptures of Israel and the interpretative logic of the rabbis. Since God was announced to Moses as the God of Abraham, Isaac and Jacob, these patriarchs must still be alive: there is indeed a resurrection.

Scribes (12.28-40)
The scribes enter the debate in the form of a single scribe whose question seems legitimate: which is the greatest of the commandments? The

answer would be known by any faithful Jew: Hear, O Israel, the Lord our God, the Lord is one, and you shall love the Lord your God with all your heart and all your soul and with all your mind and with all your strength (Deut. 6.4). The interpretative skill of Jesus is shown when he adds to it a second command, which is the application of the first: love your neighbour as yourself (Lev. 19.18).

The comments of the scribe affirm the answer of Jesus, acknowledge his role as teacher and place the comments of Jesus in a theological context. In the opinion of the scribe to obey God in the way Jesus commands is greater that the cultic acts associated with the temple: whole burnt offerings and sacrifices (12.33).

Unlike the other debates this questioner goes away with the blessings of Jesus. His wise answer shows that he is not far from the Kingdom of God. Thus Jesus has entered into the temple and taken on all comers. Not only is he able to handle the questions brought to him by the religious leaders, but he is also able to draw an earnest seeker near to the Kingdom. No more questions are asked by the leaders (12.34).

The Parable of the Vineyard (Mark 12.1-12)

In the midst of this string of debates and conflict with the religious leadership of Israel stands a parable by Jesus (12.1-9). Internally the parable is open to two interpretations, depending upon the location of the reader. If the reader thinks absentee landlords deserve income from their land, then the workers are criminals. If the reader thinks absentee landlords are unjust, then the workers are liberators.

Various keys within the parable suggest that it is to be read as a paradigm of God's history with Israel. A Jewish reader would probably recognize the vineyard as a symbol for Israel and the workers as Israel's leaders (Isa. 5.1-7). If so, the owner (lord) of the vineyard provides a clear symbol for Yahweh. The abused messengers then take on the profile of Israel's prophets; in particular the messenger wounded in the head bears the image of the Baptist. This line of messengers ends with the sending of the child of the owner, who is described as a 'beloved son' (12.6). Thus the parable becomes a clear sign of the rejection of Jesus, the beloved son (1.11; 9.7), as God's final messenger. The reader should recognize what the religious leaders in the story recognize: this parable is directed against the leaders of Israel (12.12).

This parable also adds important values to this story. The history of Israel has been interpreted, after the manner of the prophets, as one of rejection and failure. From a theological perspective God's relations with Israel are sketched in lines of judgment. A christological motif is also at work here. Jesus is the beloved son, he completes the line of the prophets and his death is a consequence of his mission.

Beyond these internal clues a reader trained in the patterns of this Gospel will see here an interpolation. The line of questioning (11.27-33; 12.13-34) has been broken by this parable. Thus the reader knows to interpret this parable through the questions and to interpret the questions through this parable. A double sign is created: the conflict over Jesus' teaching in the temple belongs to the larger story of God's working with Israel, and these scenes will end in the death of Jesus. In this way the attempts to entrap Jesus are raised to a new level of maliciousness; they are a part of a process that will lead to his death. At the same time the parable of the vineyard is moved from the realm of ideas and images into the streets of Jerusalem. In the scenes at the temple the destiny of Israel is being played out with stark clarity.

The interpretative sequence that follows the parable (12.10-11) confirms this. Using the Scriptures of Israel, Jesus insists that his rejection will be reversed and that his work will become a key component (the keystone) in God's new work.

It is precisely this interpretation of Israel's history and Jesus' destiny that stirs the arrest of Jesus (12.12). As the passion narrative (Mk 14-16) will show, Jesus' teaching in the temple provides the cause of his death.

Jesus Asks a Question (Mark 12.35-37)

While previous scenes showed the ability of Jesus to counter theological questions asked by others, this scene demonstrates the power of Jesus to pose the questions that matter. Applying a common pattern of Jewish interpretation, Jesus exegetes the message of Psalm 110 about the messiah. Though he does not apply the lesson to himself, the connection is obvious.

This scene answers the question asked in 11.28: by what authority are you doing these things? Standing in the city of David, Jesus declares from Israel's Scriptures that the messiah is lord over Davidic tradition. The first reader would know that this includes not only Jerusalem, but also a monument first conceived by David—the temple.

Jesus Issues a Warning (Mark 12.38-40)

The final public instruction is aimed at the scribes. Jesus warns his listeners about acts of self-serving piety. Most of the description presents the scribes as arrogant, but harmless, religious figures. One line suggests otherwise: they devour the houses of widows. A reader familiar with the Old Testament will know that this violates the fundamental piety of Judaism (Exod. 22.22; Isa. 10.1-3). In an echo of the parable of the vineyard (12.9), such abuse evokes God's judgment (12.40).

The Lesson from the Widow (Mark 12.41-44)

A catchword connection from Mk 12.40 ('devouring the houses of widows') leads to the story in 12.41-44. This story is also an extension of the arrogance theme from the previous verses. A second catchword connection can be found in the term for 'abundance'. Arrogant scribes will receive abundant judgment (12.40), and the rich give out of their abundance (12.44).

Jesus observes the piety of Israel at the offering box. The contrast between the gifts of the rich and the gift of the poor widow provides, for Jesus, a lesson. It also provides an occasion for private instruction of his disciples. Jesus reinterprets giving on a relative scale: she gave more because she gave all.

While this story is usually seen as a blessing on such giving, the alert reader may sense other clues. Jesus has condemned piety that seeks out its own interest, but destroys the poor and powerless. In particular those who devour the houses of widows are denounced (12.40). Since this entire act (11.1-13.37) offers condemnation of the temple, religious leaders and Israel's patterns of worship, why should this scene be any different? At least implicit in the remarks of Jesus is a critique of a religious system that would relish robes and banquets (12.38-39) and great buildings (13.1), yet take from a widow her last possessions. If this reading is secure, then the larger act opens and closes with a prophetic critique of the materialism of the Jerusalem temple (11.12-25; 12.38-40).

The location of this scene is as important as its content. Even as the healing of Bartimaeus (10.46-52) comes at the end of a long line of failure by Jesus' disciples, so the story of the widow comes at the end of Jesus' conflicts with the religious leaders. As with Bartimaeus the deeds of the widow are cast—over against the failure of others—as a model of discipleship.

Teaching on the Mount of Olives (Mark 13)

Mark 13.1-2 plays a key role in the framing of this unit. In Mk 11.27 Jesus enters the temple and is confronted by religious leaders. The teaching scenes that follow are set over against the temple and the leadership of Israel, giving voice to the vineyard drama of 11.12-25. This line of public debate closes with the departure of Jesus from the temple in 13.1. For the second time Jesus leaves the temple behind (11.11; 13.1). While the prophecy in 13.1-2 is given to his disciples and will provide the substance of ch. 13, Jesus' prediction of the fall of the temple completes the prophetic condemnation that flows through the temple scenes. Within this Gospel Jesus never returns to the temple, and it will it play no positive role in the future of his movement.

The stark prediction of the temple's destruction (13.1-2) stands in contrast to the awe of the disciples at the wondrous buildings. The teachings that follow remove the temple from any continuing role in the life of Jesus' followers.

Theological geography is used once again to set the ideological tone. Jesus' teaching to his disciples is set on the Mount of Olives, which is described as 'over against the temple' (13.3). The narrative creates a world apart for this line of instruction; it is given to disciples in private, it is set apart on a mountain and it addresses a future that lies beyond the realms of the story line.

The instruction in Mk 13.5-37 is dominated not by prediction, but by warning. The term 'look out' or 'beware' occurs four times (13.5, 9, 23, 33), the word for 'watch' occurs three times (13.34, 35, 37), one synonym for 'watch' is used (13.33). Thus the point of the prophecy is not divination, but discipleship. Even as Jesus instructed disciples in how to follow in the Galilee and Jerusalem, so he now instructs them for the future.

The context of the teaching is set by Jesus' prediction of the temple's demise, but also by the question of the disciples: when shall these things occur, and what is the sign when all of this is about to be accomplished? (13.4). The first half of this teaching unit deconstructs their expectations. The catastrophes about to happen in Jerusalem and Judaea are not the end of the world. A series of traumatic events will occur: false leaders will come in Jesus' name, wars will come, nations will war, earthquakes will shake the earth, famines will occur, believers will be persecuted, the 'desecrating abomination' will arise (13.14), unprecedented tribulations will occur, false messiahs and false prophets will arise. In the face of these tragedies a strong thematic line endures: these events do not mark the end of the age. When wars arise this is 'not yet the end' (13.7). When nation rises against nation and earthquakes and famine arise, this is 'the beginning of birthpangs' (13.8). In the face of the coming persecution 'the one enduring to the end shall be saved' (13.13).

Thus Mk 13.5-20 places the coming catastrophes, including the fall of the temple, in a realistic perspective. This time will be difficult, but it is not the end of the world. In the midst of the tragedies that will surround them followers of Jesus have work to do. First, they must maintain their own faithfulness. They are not to be led astray by false claims (13.5-6, 21-23). They must face persecution and endure to the end (13.9-13). Secondly, they are to bear witness to the gospel. They will stand before governors and kings to bear witness in behalf of Jesus (13.9). Most importantly, they are to preach the gospel to all the nations (13.10).

Disciples of Jesus are to take the traumatic events of the future as a call to steadfastness and service. These events will mark not the end, but the beginning of a worldwide mission for the gospel. Finally, disciples are to flee from Judaea when they see these events underway (13.14-16).

While this message is addressed in the narrative to Peter, James, John and Andrew, the real audience lies beyond the frame of the story. Those who experience the fall of Jerusalem some 40 years hence should find here their marching orders. While this is evident from the tone of the text, one intrusion by the narrator confirms this rhetoric. 'Let the reader understand!', says the narrator in response to the 'desolating sacrilege' (13.14). But Jesus had no readers. This prophecy, like all of Jesus' teaching, was delivered in oral form and was long transmitted in the frame of orality. This message is clearly addressed to the first *reader*, who lives in the 70s in the aftermath of the first Jewish War.

Mark 13.1-20 thus demonstrates the complexity of this Gospel and its ability to create various levels of signification and communication. In the aftermath of the temple controversies, a new place is created for Jesus' instruction, a new time is embraced and a new audience is addressed. All of these events belong to the earthly, historical plane, giving the readers who listens over the shoulder of the disciples clear instruction for the tasks of their own age. Those who heed this warning will not only survive and endure; they will take the gospel to the nations.

The second half of this unit moves beyond earthly events and historical time. The allusion to the Old Testament (Joel 2.10; Isa. 13.10; 34.4) sets these prophecies in cosmological perspective:

> The sun shall be darkened, and the moon shall not give its light.
> The stars will be falling from the heaven, and the powers in the heavens
> shall be shaken (Joel 2.10).

These astrological events precede the appearance of the son of man. In an image drawn from the prophet Daniel, the son of man will come in clouds with much power and glory. He will then send forth his angels to gather the elect, an image also drawn from the Old Testament (Zech. 2.6; Deut. 30.4; Isa. 43.5-11).

This vision of the future is also set within close bounds. First, its images are rooted in selected Old Testament passages, preventing unbounded speculation. Secondly, the prediction is short on specifics. Thirdly, the timing of this process is unknown, even to the angels or the son (13.32). Fourthly, even this event is drawn into the earthly dimensions of discipleship. How are disciples to prepare for this cosmological phenomenon? They are to observe the fig tree and to learn its lessons (13.28). They are to expect these events as a part of their own age

(13.30). They are to watch in preparation (13.33-37). The spectacular events of Mk 13.24-27 are thus framed in scriptural images and in earthly parables (13.28-29, 34) and pronouncements (13.30, 31, 32), then directed to the task of discipleship.

Thus this Gospel does not abandon its standard forms nor its central focus in light of the future events. Through various literary techniques these future events are connected to the earthly mission of Jesus and to the continuing demands for discipleship. These connections will be strengthened and clarified in the scenes of the passion story (Mk 14-16).

The Story Thus Far

While the first three acts (1.21-3.7a; 3.7-6.6; 6.6b-8.27a) established the ministry of Jesus in the Galilee, the fourth act (8.27-10.52) described the difficulty of discipleship and defined Jesus as one who suffers and serves and dies. The fifth act of this Gospel (11.1-13.37) shapes the story to the ethos of a new setting—Jerusalem. The conflict between Jesus and the religious leadership of Israel dominates these scenes. Various literary forms demonstrate this conflict: a prophetic scene in the temple (11.15-19); an enigmatic miracle story (11.12-14, 20-25); a series of debates (11.27-12.40); a parable (12.1-12); a paradigm (12.41-44); pronouncements against the temple (13.1-2).

This conflict offers a carefully developed critique of Israel's worship, but much more is added to the story by these units. The plot line becomes clear: the teaching of Jesus, particularly in relation to the temple, will lead to his death. The characterization of Jesus is given new focus. His teaching in Jerusalem surpasses the wisdom of Israel's leaders. He will suffer and die for the people. His story is a part of the larger work of God with Israel, and his rejection and death belongs to Israel's history of rejection and failure.

An important new component has broken into the world of the story—and the world of the reader. This new thing profoundly affects the setting, the plotting and the characterization of this Gospel. The time beyond Jesus' death has been brought into the story. The gospel has been set in a worldwide context. The events of the first Jewish War have been integrated. The end of the age has been envisioned. New lines have also been added to the characterization of Jesus. In this act Jesus has been declared to be the son of man who will be raised from death and will come with the clouds of heaven to gather his elect from the ends of the earth.

Through these scenes an important line of prophecy has been put into place. Some prophecies can only be fulfilled in the distant future.

Other events will unfold, after the Jewish War, in the lives of the first readers. The events predicted for Jesus' own life will come to reality in the final act (Mk 14-16). The conflict developed by Mk 11.1-13.37 will be played out in the passion narrative.

Mark 14.1-42:
The Preparation and Betrayal

The first section of the passion narrative extends from Mk 14.1-42 and contains four units (14.1-11; 14.12-26; 14.26-32a; 14.32-42). Composing the sixth act of this Gospel, these four stories play a vital role in the account of Jesus' death. The passion story is initiated and embodied by a private anointing (14.1-11). The Passover meal (14.12-26) joins images from the Old Testament to the death of Jesus. The prediction of betrayal (14.26-32a) points to the events ahead. The scene in Gethsemane (14.32-42) sets the stage for the arrest and trial of Jesus. These scenes in Jerusalem generate the plot line of the passion story and create a vivid portrait of Jesus.

The Anointing Story (Mark 14.1-11)

From a literary and theological perspective the scene in Mk 14.1-11 is marked by unusual complexity. Located at the juncture of Jesus' ministry and his death, the anointing story is pivotal for both plot and characterization.

A key theme of this unit is the plan to arrest and execute Jesus. The conspiracy of 14.1-2 matches precisely the images of 11.18: priests and scribes seek to kill Jesus but are hindered by the volatility of the people. The opening lines (14.1) create an ironic setting: in the sacred season of Passover the Jewish leaders plot the death of Jesus.

The conspiracy theme is completed in Mk 14.10-11. One of the Twelve makes an agreement for money to hand Jesus over to the religious leaders. The irony is deepened: Jesus will be handed over to death by one of his own.

While Mk 14.10-11 could easily follow 14.1-2, the conspiracy has been broken open and set as a frame around the anointing scene in Mk 14.3-9. This scene could also stand by itself: it has a new setting, a new cast of characters, a different ethos and a different style of narration. The action at the centre of this scene is minimal: a woman breaks a flask of nard and anoints the head of Jesus (14.3). The characterization of the woman is flat: she is not named and she does not speak. The real centre of the unit is found in the extended dialogue about her actions.

Some grumble about the waste of the perfume and chastise the woman. The first reader, who would know the perfume cost the equivalent of a year's wage, might agree. The complaint of the observers sets in motion a series of four disparate sayings from Jesus. The first two sayings are given a logical coherence. The first saying (14.6) designates the anointing not as a wasteful deed deserving reprimand, but as a 'good work'. The first reader would know that such deeds are foundational in Jewish piety. The second saying (14.7-8a) acknowledges the validity of giving in behalf of the poor, which is also a good work, but relativizes almsgiving in view of Jesus' presence. While some acts of love may be valued even above giving to the poor, the point here is christological: she has done extravagantly what can be done only once for the departing messiah.

The third and fourth sayings have no logical connection in this scene. The third saying (14.8b) introduces the burial theme and links it to the woman's deeds. The fourth saying (14.9) addresses the theme of the gospel and missionary proclamation. The connection of the woman's deed to the burial of Jesus and to the spread of the gospel are not logical, but theological: they are imposed upon her act by the words of Jesus. The pronouncement in 14.9 is an Amen-saying, placing it among four such sayings which are linked to the death of Jesus (14.9, 18, 25, 30).

The reader is invited to compare this scene to the offering of the widow in Mk 12.41-44. Both are silent witnesses who gave what they had (12.44) or did what they could (14.8). Both are presented by Jesus as paradigms of discipleship. The careful reader might also remember that the preaching of the gospel to the world (14.9) is a part of the eschatological scenario of ch. 13 (13.10).

The complexity and nuance of this account becomes apparent. In the inner scene the simple act of a silent woman has been given coherence and significance through the words of Jesus. This inner scene (14.3-9) has been framed by a conspiracy (14.1-2, 10-11), creating a study in contrasts. While the characters in the introduction and conclusion are marked by religious standing (chief priests, scribes, one of the Twelve), the centre of the story is inhabited by characters of low esteem. The religious leaders represent Jerusalem; the anointing takes place in Bethany. Chief priests occupy the temple—the house of God—while Jesus occupies the house of a leper. Religious leaders perform the sacred symbolic rites of Israel; chief among these is the approaching Passover meal. In contrast, a woman slips into Jesus' meal with Simon and performs a rite reserved for kings and priests and prophets. The compassion of this woman inverts the deeds of Judas and the religious leaders and provides a sharp alternative to the hostility of the outer scene.

Lest the reader miss this relationship, these colliding worlds are connected by two narrative threads. The money motif plays a secondary role in both sections (14.5, 11). A more important connection is established around the motif of Jesus' passion. Both scenes portray people who will accompany Jesus to his death. One group accompanies Jesus with hostility, conspiracy, betrayal; an unnamed woman accompanies Jesus with extravagant compassion and insight. This strategy gathers the whole of Mk 14.1-11 into a narrative piece marked by vivid contrast.

Beyond its local impact as a complex literary and theological construction, the scene in Mk 14.1-11 plays an important role in the structuring of the passion story. While Luke places this story in the midst of Jesus' ministry with no reference to the passion (Lk. 7.36-50), the saying in Mk 14.8 casts the anointing into the larger stream of the passion story.

The anointing scene also plays a key role in the larger flow of this Gospel. The location of the story is important for two reasons. First, the location of Mk 14.1-11 makes it part of the frame for the entire passion narrative. Mark 16.1-8 concludes the passion account with the puzzling story of women who are unsuccessful in their attempt to anoint Jesus and of a message that they fail to proclaim. In contrast Mk 14.1-11 prefaces the passion account with the story of a woman who successfully anoints Jesus and of a message proclaimed in all the world. Secondly, this scene is located at the juncture between Jesus' public ministry and his death. Mark 14.1-11 is the last public act of Jesus' ministry, and it introduces the passion account.

In addition to its location other images connect this story to the wider narrative world. (1) The rejection experienced by Jesus throughout his ministry emerges anew in the form of hostile leaders (14.1-2), insensitive critics (14.4-5) and unfaithful followers (14.10-11). (2) Jesus' fellowship with common people is reflected in this scene, where he is hosted by a leper and anointed by a woman. (3) The faithful discipleship of minor characters is repeated in the deeds of this unnamed woman. (4) The eschatological urgency that marks Jesus' mission can be seen in his suspension of normal rules of piety (14.7). (5) The theme of the gospel is taken up and given new dimensions in this scene. Standing at a crucial juncture in the narrative, this story gathers up various components of Jesus' public ministry and casts them under the interpretive framework of his death.

These connections provide a reading strategy—a hermeneutic—for the reader of this Gospel. Mark 14.1-11 insists that the passion narrative cannot stand alone as an independent account, since the passion account is deeply rooted in the story of Jesus' words and deeds. In the same way, the words and deeds of Jesus are brought under the final interpretative frame of his death and resurrection.

At the centre of these narrative transactions stands a distinct line of characterization. Through its primary emphasis on the sayings material, Mk 14.1-11 gives sharp focus to the role of Jesus as teacher and prophet. His pronouncements reveal the true meaning of present events and prophesy the shape of the future. The authoritative teacher/prophet now stands in view of his own death. He is hated by religious leaders and betrayed by one of the Twelve. In contrast he is welcomed by the lowly, who share his fellowship. Jesus is here presented as God's anointed, but it is his death which provides the singular key to his messianic identity. Such stories of Jesus are a part of the gospel story that will be proclaimed in all the world.

The Passover Meal (Mark 14.12-26)

The story of the Passover meal has been constructed around three distinct narrative segments (14.12-16; 14.17-21; 14.22-26). Each of these units opens with a temporal marker: the day of Passover (14.12); when evening had come (14.17); while they were eating (14.22). The first segment refers to the followers of Jesus as disciples, while the other two speak of the Twelve.

The central segment (14.17-21) stands in relative independence from the other two. Nothing in this meal directly picks up the Passover theme. Within 14.17-21 only the mention of the cup in 14.20 deals with the meal. The focus on the meal falls to the background, and three sayings from Jesus are placed in the foreground (14.18, 20, 21). Three themes dominate these sayings: betrayal, discipleship failure, the handing over of the son of man. Sandwiched between the first saying ('One of you eating with me will betray me') and the second saying ('One of the Twelve who dips with me in the cup') is a stark query from the each of the disciples: 'It is not me, is it?' (14.19). The effect of this is to magnify the charge. Through this query the unthinkable prophecy of 14.18 is repeated twelvefold: Jesus will be handed over by one of his followers. The third saying (14.21) takes up the standard form of the 'handing over' prophecy: as in 9.31; 10.33; 14.41 'the son of man is handed over'. Building around this standard formula, this third saying develops this prophecy: (1) the one handed over is, for the first time in the passion story, identified as the son of man; (2) his going up fulfils the Scriptures; (3) the betrayal of the son of man is a crime for which the betrayer stands condemned.

Mark 14.22-26 could also stand as an independent unit: it has its own set of time and place markers (14.22). Again there is no clear reference to a Passover meal. This segment is structured around the meal elements, but it is focused around the sayings material. The first saying

(14.22c) identifies the bread with the body of Jesus, but offers no further explanation. The second saying (14.24) similarly interprets the cup as the blood of Jesus. Only in the last part of the second saying is the significance of the bread and wine established: the death of Jesus establishes a new covenant, and this covenant is for 'the many'. The first reader should recognize here a reformulation of the exodus covenant. The participation of 'all' in this covenant meal contrasts the subsequent failure of 'all' in 14.27 and 14.50. The final saying (14.25) links the death of Jesus to the coming of the Kingdom. The hymn (14.26) has been used as a dismissal scene, and the departure to the Mount of Olives will be important for the following scenes.

A typical meal scene provides the stage for a series of pronouncements by Jesus. These sayings set his own death in the context of the betrayal by one, the failure by all and the handing over of the son of man. More importantly the elements of a typical meal are transformed into signs of the new covenant and the coming Kingdom.

The opening segment in Mk 14.12-16 casts this meal as a Passover. In this way the images that emerged from Jesus' meal with his followers are now linked to the larger story of Israel. The alert reader will note that this preparation is remarkably similar to the preparation before entering Jerusalem (Mk 11.1-6). The preparation sequence in 14.12-16 suggests that Jesus has prophetic foresight, and his status as the Teacher is highlighted (14.14). In addition, the expectation of a guest room is common in prophetic stories (1 Kgs 18.17-24; 2 Kgs 4.8-17). Thus the final meal of Jesus is significant not only for his followers, who here learn the significance of his death; it is also important for 'the many' of Israel. A teacher and prophet has come to Jerusalem and a new covenant—a new Kingdom—is being established.

Through these narrative moves this scene defines—before the event—the significance of Jesus' death. This understanding is available to all who sit at the table—and to all who listen over their shoulders.

The Prophecy of Betrayal (Mark 14.26-32a)

The prophecy of betrayal is played out between the departure from the meal (14.26) and the arrival in Gethsemane (14.32a). This frame creates a single, stable episode. The scene is devoid of action. It presents instead a heated debate between Jesus and his disciples. Within this short span four sayings from Jesus (14.27a, 27b, 28, 29) are countered by responses from Peter and others (14.29, 31b, c, 31d). This point–counterpoint dialogue develops two thematic lines. Most of the sayings and rebuttals centre on a 'scandalized' theme. This theme is given precise focus through the words of Jesus (14.27a), then heightened through three cycles of development. This line of debate is concerned primarily for the destiny of the disciples and only consequently with the impact upon Jesus. This theme dominates the flow of Mk 14.26-32a and controls its level of intensity.

The second theme is developed around the image of the shepherd (14.27b-28). The shepherd/sheep imagery echoes the prophetic word in Zech. 13.7, and this connection is made explicit by the citation formula ('it stands written'). This second theme gives primary attention to the destiny of Jesus, with consequent concern for his followers. While this prophecy is rooted in the Old Testament, it has been extended into the future with unusual specificity: Jesus will be raised and will go before the disciples into the Galilee.

This prophecy in 14.27b-28 reshapes the entire episode, realigns the plot line and sharpens the portrait of Jesus. In so doing a dramatic stream of hope is unleashed. In the midst of total, unrelieved failure stands a prophetic image of Jesus. The flow of the 'scandalized' theme is met by the counterflow of the shepherd theme. The collapse of the disciples is met by the promise of the Risen One. The debacle which is about to occur in Jerusalem is countered by the promise of the Galilee.

Gethsemane (Mark 14.32-42)

The transition that opens and closes the Gethsemane story (14.32, 42) delineates a scene of prayer and abandonment. Structurally this account is built around three cycles of instruction–prayer–return. Through a pattern of reduction the disciples are reduced from the larger group (14.32) to the three (14.33), then to Jesus alone (14.35, 39). The pattern of instruction–prayer–return is also reduced from a full report (14.32b-38) to summary reports (14.39-40, 41). This reduction focuses the scene and intensifies its impact upon the isolated characters. The repetition of the instruction–prayer–return pattern, though in reduced form, creates narrative emphasis.

Two thematic lines flow through this scene: the failure of the disciples and the faithfulness of Jesus. These themes are not explicit in the events of the story, but are developed through various literary techniques. At first reading one finds here nothing more than a simple story of human frailty. After a late meal, including wine, the disciples grow sleepy. The framing and telling of this story has elevated the scene into a decisive moment of faith and failure.

The inner scenes of Jesus at prayer (14.32, 34a, 35-36) have been carefully tuned to the characterization of Jesus. The tradition of Jesus' lament/prayer employs numerous images that are infrequent in this

Gospel, but are foundational to the early Christian tradition. The address of God as Abba (Father) reflects a strong liturgical tradition tied to sonship (Rom. 8.15; Gal. 4.6) as well as the Lord's Prayer tradition (Mt. 6.9; Lk. 11.2). The confession that 'all things are possible' echoes a Christian tradition found in various forms and contexts (Mk 11.22-26; Mt. 17.20; Lk. 17.6; 1 Cor. 13.2). The symbolic use of the cup is widespread in early Christianity. The metaphorical use of 'the hour' as a decisive moment of judgment or death has numerous parallels, especially in the Gospel of John. The lament of Mk 14.34 is based on allusion to various Old Testament psalms (Pss. 42.5, 6, 11; 43.5, for example). Thus the inner scene of Jesus' experience in Gethsemane seems to be framed in the wider language and images of early Christian tradition.

The christological theme embedded in the inner sanctum of this story (14.32, 34a, 35-36) helps to define the intensity of this moment. (1) Jesus is portrayed as the faithful son who watches with prayer and obedience. (2) The presence of the son transforms the call to watch and pray from general admonition to an urgent necessity. (3) The presence of 'the hour' transforms the temptation (14.38) from a general warning to a stark danger of failure. (4) This impending sense of eschatological urgency and the need to watch and pray is linked directly to the suffering and death of Jesus. (5) The eschatological 'hour' (14.41) is linked directly to the 'hour' of Jesus' suffering (14.35). Through these transactions the scene of a faithful Jew at prayer is transformed. General warnings become christological and eschatological imperatives. The critical urgency of this hour is linked directly to the suffering of Jesus, the obedient son.

These inner transactions shed new light on the disciples' response. While the role of the outer group is unfocused—they are commanded only to sit (14.32)—they are guilty by association. More meaningful commands are given to the three—remain and watch (14.34), watch and pray (14.35)—and their failure is focused more precisely—sleeping (14.37), weakness of the flesh (14.38), heavy eyes (14.40), inability to speak (14.40). While these may appear, at face value, to be typical human behaviour, the inner scene of Jesus at prayer casts them in new proportions.

The focus on discipleship failure (14.33, 34b, 37-41a, b) serves as a host for various other concerns and transactions. The focused commands to the three ('remain and watch', 14.34) and to Peter ('watch and pray', 14.38) provide sufficient grounds for the charge against the disciples. The sleeping of the disciples is developed into a charge, since it also represents a failure to watch and pray. Such sleep is here associated with temptation and weakness. It impairs the vision of the disciples and leaves them mute. Thus a typical biological response has been transformed into a deadly failure. The addition of 'until death' (14.34) to the line from Psalm 42 raises the level of Jesus' sorrow and suffering and intensifies the failure of the disciples. Because their sleeping has been cast in a new light, this danger becomes the subject of Jesus' teaching on human need in general (14.34, 38). This danger is applied most specifically to Peter, who is now addressed by the name (Simon) he used before his call to follow Jesus. Through these trans-actions, the sleep of the disciples is defined as a moral flaw and spiritual danger indicative of human existence. This failure of the disciples to watch with Jesus is defined as a complete fall and an absolute abandon-ment of identity.

The two themes—the failure of the disciples and the faithfulness of Jesus—are united in the final lines of the story (14.41c-42). The two streams that flow through the Gethsemane scene converge in one stark, tense saying: 'It is done. The hour has come.' The failure of the disciples is ensured, and the destiny of the son is decided.

The reader who has learned the codes of this Gospel will know that the Gethsemane scene culminates a long line of development in plot and characterization. The son who is beloved of God (1.11; 9.7; 12.6) has taught with authority the coming of God's Reign. The controversy stirred by this teaching is leading to his death. Those whom he called to follow (1.16-20; 3.13-19) have struggled throughout, and now their fail-ure is complete.

Since this Gospel is presented as a text, the reader is invited to read not only sequentially, but also reflectively. The alert reader will recognize that the Gethsemane scene is intricately linked to the wider story of the Gospel and plays a key role in its interpretation. (1) While the failure of the disciples in 14.32-42 is teased from a common human response, this failure to watch and understand is part of a consistent, extended pattern in this Gospel. (2) While the theme of betrayal emerges only at the end of the Gethsemane scene (14.41, 42) and is not directly related to their sleep, the final prophetic word of 14.41 unites a long line of images and predictions of abandonment (3.6; 8.31; 9.31; 10.32-34; 14.18, 20; 14.27, 28, 30). (3) The portrait of Jesus in the Gethsemane scene takes up numerous images from Mk 1-13: the obedient son, the son of man, the passion Christology. (4) Numerous links tie the Gethsemane story to the inappropriate request from the disciples in Mk 10.35-40: the sons of Zebedee, the cup, the able/not able contrast, not knowing what to ask or what to answer, the connection of these scenes to the passion. Through these connections the arrogant request of 10.35-40 foreshadows the dangers and the demands of discipleship—a prophecy realized in

14.32-42. (5) The naming of Peter in the Gethsemane scene takes on new significance in connection with the wider narrative. When he was appointed as the first of the Twelve, Simon was named as Peter, the rock. In congruence with the Old Testament, a new calling suggests a new name. The reversion to the name Simon in the Gethsemane scene (14.37) suggests a narrative reversal of Peter's appointment and the abandonment of his identity and vocation. (6) The Gethsemane scene has strong ties to the transfiguration story in Mk 9.2-10: the calling apart of disciples, the mountain setting, the three, a change in Jesus' demeanour, Peter as the representative of the Twelve, the use of triads, the disciples do not know what to answer Jesus, Jesus is designated son of God, the son of man title is used in connection with Jesus' death, both scenes are framed by the impotence of the disciples. This extensive line of connections unveils for the reader a decisive hermeneutic: every vision of the son of God and the son of man must be filtered through the experience of Jesus' suffering and death.

Most significantly, the Gethsemane story provides a hermeneutic for reading the enigmatic scenes of Mark 13. Numerous connections are established between the stark prayer scene in Gethsemane and the apocalyptic images of Mark 13:

1. The inner circle of three is central to both scenes (13.3; 14.33);
2. The theme of betrayal is important (13.9, 11, 12; 14.41, 42);
3. The concept of the 'hour' is employed (13.11, 32; 14.35, 41);
4. Endurance is the sign of true discipleship (13.13; 14.34);
5. Death is important in both accounts (13.12; 14.34);
6. In both scenes disciples are commanded to pray (13.18; 14.38);
7. Both stories employ the image of sleep (13.36; 14.37, 40, 41);
8. The image of the son of man stands at the centre of both scenes (13.26; 14.41);
9. The command to watch provides the primary exhortation in both units (13.5, 9, 33, 34, 35, 37; 14.34, 37, 38).

These narrative links suggest that Mark 13 should be read in view of Mk 14.32-42. Through these connections the Gethsemane scene helps to draw the apocalyptic images of Mark 13 into the mainstream of the Gospel. The son of man who will come in glory is also the son of man who is handed over to sinners, the prophet who moves consciously toward his own death.

Conversely Mark 13 impacts the reading of the Gethsemane story, as well as the entire passion account. While Gethsemane ends in failure and betrayal, the reader now knows the future of the suffering son of man: he will come with power and glory.

The Story Thus Far

The four scenes in Mk 14.1-42 prove crucial to the story of Jesus' death and to the wider Gospel story. These scenes are all set in Jerusalem and the surrounding areas. Leaving behind the controversy in the temple, Jesus moves from the house of a leper to an upper room to the Mount of Olives to Gethsemane. These geographical settings carry with them a stark ethos: in the city where he will meet his death Jesus is surrounded by hostility, betrayal, rejection, abandonment.

While the plot line of this Gospel has been dominated by fast-paced action, this act has little real action. Even the ordinary actions—anointing the head, breaking bread, drinking wine, sleeping, praying—are secondary to the sayings that dominate this act. Nonetheless Mk 14.1-42 provides two important plot functions: prediction and symbol. Each of the stories speaks of future events crucial to the story: the suffering, death and burial of Jesus; the worldwide gospel mission; the betrayal; the coming Kingdom; abandonment by the Twelve; the arrest of Jesus. At the same time these accounts create various narrative symbols: anointing, bread, wine, the shepherd, the sheep, the cup, the hour. These stories serve as narrative prophecies that predict and embody the death of Jesus.

These stories also play a key role in the characterization of Jesus. Central to each account is the image of Jesus as one who dies for the cause of God. Other images of Jesus also emerge from these scenes: he is a true and reliable prophet, the teacher and shepherd of God's people. He is hated by religious leaders, betrayed and abandoned by disciples, but welcomed and loved by outcasts and sinners. Jesus is the founder of a new covenant, the son of man who brings the Kingdom. Jesus is the innocent sufferer, the obedient son, the fulfilment of the Scriptures. Each of these christological images is carved against a second line of characterization—the failure, abandonment and betrayal by the disciples.

This act also puts in place an important schema of prophecy/ fulfilment. Through his pronouncements Jesus offers numerous claims about the future. Some things predicted by Jesus have immediate fulfilment, as in the preparation for Passover (14.12-16). Other events predicted by Jesus, such as his betrayal, are already under way. Many things predicted by Jesus are about to be accomplished in Jerusalem. Some things predicted by Jesus (13.1-37; 14.28) can only be fulfilled beyond the realms of the story.

The reader is not simply an observer of these predictions; the reader is being instructed in the reliability of these pronouncements. When the reader learns that Jesus' plans for the Passover happen as he predicted, a contract of confidence is established. As the reader sees other predicted events come to pass, this confidence is affirmed. When the disciples abandon Jesus and the numerous passion predictions begin to unfold, the role of Jesus as God's true prophet will be established. The step-by-step instruction that begins in this act will prove crucial for the reading of this Gospel. Ultimately the appearance of the Risen One and the coming of the son of man lie outside the world of the story as unfulfilled prophecy. Because the invested reader has learned elsewhere to read the pronouncements of Jesus with confidence, these future events can also be embraced as reliable prophecy. Through these complex strategies the narrative prepares the reader to deal with the scandalous death of Jesus and with the future unleashed by this story.

Mark 14.43-15.15: The Arrest and Trial

Mark 14.43-15.15 provides the second major section of the passion narrative and the seventh act of this Gospel. Through four scenes (14.43-53a; 14.53-65; 14.66-72; 15.1-15) this act narrates the betrayal and arrest, the denial by Peter and the two trials scenes.

Betrayal, Arrest, Abandonment (Mark 14.43-53a)

Mark 14.43-53a narrates the betrayal by Judas, the arrest by religious authorities and the abandonment by disciples. A process of representation is at work in this passage. Judas is introduced as 'one of the Twelve' (14.43). The crowd is sent from the religious leaders (14.43). The option of violence is represented by one bystander (14.47). The abandonment by Jesus' followers is exemplified in the flight of the naked youth (14.51-52). This scene is constituted around two action sequences (14.43-47; 14.50-53a) and a series of pronouncements (14.48-49).

The first action sequence is framed in 14.43-47. The opening motif assumes the presence of Jesus and the disciples, then invokes the presence of Judas, the mob and the religious leaders. The comment of the narrator (14.44) explains Judas's prearranged signal and completes the preparation for the scene. The staccato sequence of action that follows provides the basic plot structure for the story. Numerous elements from this scene become poignant symbols—the Twelve, a kiss, the rabbi title, the sword. This curt sequence initiates a stream of violent betrayal, seizure, abandonment.

The second action sequence (14.50-53a) provides the transition that closes the scene. This departure, which is a typical closing motif, is accomplished through sharply contrasting images. All of the followers flee from the scene. While this seems to represent the ultimate degree of abandonment, 14.51-52 duplicates this abandonment with increased precision and intensity—a solitary follower flees naked into the night. In stark contrast to the flight of the followers, the departure of Jesus is a forced procession to judgment and death (14.53a).

The two action sequences (14.43-47; 14.50-53a) that sustain the plot line also produce a prophetic focus. The story opens in the midst of Jesus' instructions. The arrival of Judas, the betrayer, provides immediate fulfilment of the prediction in 14.42. The listing of the religious authorities (14.53b) matches exactly the passion prediction of 8.31. The flight of Jesus' followers fulfils the prophecy of 14.27 and the words of Zech. 13.7. The flight of the naked youth echoes the prophecy of Amos 2.16. The abandonment of the prophet reflects an Old Testament pattern (Exod. 16.2-3; Num. 12.1-8; 1 Kgs 19.10, 14; Jer. 26.8, for example). Consequently the action sequences characterize Jesus as the end of a long line of prophets who suffer violence at the hands of the people.

A second stream emerges from the pronouncement sequence in Mk 14.48-49. In contrast to the plot function of 14.43-47 and 14.50-53a, this pronouncement sequence functions in the realm of characterization.

Three sayings are united in this segment. The first (14.48b) operates against an Old Testament backdrop and describes the scene of arrest as a violent seizure. The second saying (14.49a, b) invokes the image of Jesus teaching in the temple. This emphasis insists that the message of Jesus is no secret revolution, and his teaching 'by day' contrasts the arrest at night. The saying also notes that they did not arrest him in the public setting of the temple. The third pronouncement (14.49c) provides, in broken language, an enigmatic fulfilment formula. What events fulfil the Scripture is unclear, and which text is fulfilled is equally uncertain. Nonetheless the story insists that these events fulfil Israel's Scripture. Confirmation of this claim is left to the reader.

The pronouncement sequence in 14.48-49 adds nothing to the plot structure, but it proves crucial for the characterization of Jesus. Further support is given here to the image of Jesus as God's prophet. The numbering of Jesus among the thieves echoes an image from Isa. 53.12. Jesus' teaching in the temple and his subsequent arrest invoke the model of Jeremiah, who, following his temple sermon (Jer. 7.1-15), is also arrested (Jer. 26.8-9). The fulfilment formula also links Jesus to the prophetic tradition. The proverb of Mk 6.4 may also be heard here: a prophet is not without honour except among his own people. Thus the sayings collected in Mk 14.48-49 invoke a host of allusions and images to focus the role of Jesus as the rejected prophet of God.

The three disparate sayings collaborate in a pronouncement sequence that focuses Jesus' prophetic identity. The sayings collection is embedded within a plotted sequence of betrayal, seizure, abandonment. Through this composition the scene offers the reader a pre-trial judgment upon the identity and destiny of Jesus.

The reader who has followed the flow of the larger Gospel is invited to connect this scene to other parts of Jesus' story. In particular the arrest and betrayal of Jesus should be connected to the dramatic condemnation of the temple in Mk 11.15-19. The one who implies that the temple is in the hands of thieves (11.17) is here handed over as a thief in the night (14.48). The reader should remember that the temple drama stirred the conspiracy by religious leaders (11.18), and the reader will soon learn that Jesus' stance on the temple provides the charge for his death (14.58; 15.29).

The reader should also make the connection between the arrest scene and the parable of the vineyard (Mk 12.1-12). Whether symbolized in the vineyard (12.1) or the temple (14.49), the leaders of Israel have rejected the messenger from God. From the vineyard parable the reader knows that this rejected prophet is the beloved son (12.6) and that those who put him to death face the judgment of God (12.9).

In this manner Mk 11.15-19 and 12.1-12 provide depth and texture for the betrayal scene. The death of Jesus is tied precisely to his prophetic words and deeds and to the hostility that they produce. The linkage of the three scenes defines and reinforces the characterization of Jesus in a way that no one of these stories could do alone. The reader of this Gospel should have learned by now that no one title or image or scene can tell the full story of Jesus. Only the reading—and re-reading—of the entire Gospel can begin to do that.

The First Trial (Mark 14.53-65)

Mark 14.53-65 tells of the first trial. Because of the nature of the material a distinct, complex introduction is required. Jesus is brought forward by force; the chief priests, scribes and elders gather, and Peter follows along from a distance. The introduction of Peter is distinct, for he plays no role in the trial scene. This introduction sets the stage for the following scene in which Peter denies Jesus (15.66-72).

Mark 14.53-65 is built around a singular line of plotted action (14.53-59, 63-65) and a concentrated dialogue sequence (14.60-62). The action sequence creates a simple plot frame: Jesus is led to the high priest, the Sanhedrin seeks testimony to support a death sentence, the verdict is given, Jesus is abused. Numerous details and images fill out this basic account: the gathering of the Sanhedrin, the temple charge, the high priest's outburst, the details of the abuse. The intrusive description of Peter's presence breaks the flow of the scene and invokes a new cast of characters (Peter and the servants) and a new setting (the fire outside in the courtyard). Despite this interruption the tale of Peter is not a part of the trial scene. The result of the action sequence is a clear plot line marked by condemnation and abuse.

A dialogical cluster (14.60-62) has been woven into this action sequence. This sayings material is built around two question–answer cycles. The first cycle (14.60-61a) presents the high priest as Jesus' interlocutor. The initial query is general and ambiguous, and it evokes no response from Jesus. In contrast, the second cycle (14.61b-62) is specific and evokes a dramatic response from Jesus and the leaders. The focus of the second cycle shifts from the question of Jesus' deeds to the question of his identity. The blunt inquiry by the high priest—'Are you the Christ, the son of the Blessed One?'—is met by two stark pronouncements from Jesus. The 'I am' response invokes the name of God (Exod. 3.13-15) and provides radical affirmation of the titles used by the high priest. This claim is extended by a second pronouncement which is based on Dan. 7.13 and Ps. 110.1: 'You shall see the son of man seated at the right hand of power and coming with the clouds of heaven.' While the first question–answer cycle serves a preparatory role, the verbal cluster climaxes in the stark pronouncements of 14.62.

Thus Mk 14.53-65 constitutes a single episode with two different focal points. A basic frame is developed into a sequence of plotted action. This action sequence focuses the condemnation of Jesus at the hands of religious authorities. Operating within this sequence and serving as its summit is a dialogical sequence which focuses the identity of Jesus. The resulting scene of judgment is an important part of the passion account and proves central to the question of Jesus' identity.

This scene presents a drama in which Israel judges one of its own. When he questions and condemns Jesus, the chief priest may be understood to speak for the nation, or at least for its religious structures. The process of the trial is noteworthy. Various witnesses are called, but their testimony is shown to be false and without power to condemn. The temple charge is mentioned, but it is defused. In the place of these efforts the story gives central focus to the exchange between Jesus and the chief priest. Jesus will be judged not on the testimony of others, but upon his own witness. The central charge is blasphemy—making a false claim in relation to God. The judgment is meted out in three stages: the condemnation by the chief priest, the death sentence by the entire group, the torture by the guards.

The drama of this trial is played out against numerous Old Testament images: Israel's judgment of one of its own people; the blasphemy charge and resulting death sentence; prophetic confrontation with Israel's leaders; the evaluation of false prophecy; the rending of the garments as a sign of horror. Through these images the scene of judgment between Jesus and the chief priest reflects the heritage of Israel.

The most important product of this scene is its portrait of Jesus. The prophetic image developed in earlier stories comes to full expression here. Jesus is portrayed as one who claims to speak for God, and the trial focuses on the validity of this claim. Various elements within the scene confirm the prophetic claim: witnesses say he predicted the fall of the temple, Jesus predicts the coming of the son of man, he offers the fulfilment of Scripture. Lest the reader miss this imagery, those who torture Jesus mock him with this demand: 'Prophesy!' (14.65). Jesus, through his own words and deeds, has claimed to speak for Yahweh. This claim is rejected by the religious leaders of Israel, and Jesus is condemned to death as a false prophet who blasphemes the name of God.

The trial scene asserts other christological images. Jesus affirms the claim that he is the messiah and the son of God. Extending this imagery through Old Testament citations, Jesus also identifies himself with the son of man.

The religious leaders do not miss these claims, nor their implications. If Jesus' claims are correct then his prophetic rebuke of Israel's leadership is also true. Conversely if the chief priest is the true leader of Israel and speaks God's truth, then Jesus is a false prophet who is worthy of death. The verdict is immediate, it is decisive and it is unanimous.

The careful reader who has followed this Gospel from its beginning will find here a decisive moment in the narrative. Mark 14.62 does precisely what the rest of the Gospel of Mark has refused to do—it places explicit christological claims on the lips of Jesus. In previous developments the messianic identity is veiled from the characters in this Gospel. While a part of this motif is a traditional element in miracle stories, a significant portion of this secrecy is used to explain to later readers the widespread failure to recognize Jesus as messiah during his ministry. The Gospel of Mark makes extended use of this secrecy motif (Mk 1.24-25, 34, 44; 3.11-12; 4.11-12; 7.36; 8.26, 30; 9.9). While demons and even disciples sometimes articulate christological claims (Mk 1.24; 3.11-12; 8.27-30), Jesus distances himself from these attempts to make public his identity.

The pronouncement in Mk 14.62 provides a dramatic reversal of this pattern. Here the messianic secrecy is broken open in the presence of religious leaders and other witnesses. The hesitant acceptance of christological titles is replaced by the definitive 'I am' on the lips of Jesus. In one brief stroke the trial scene makes explicit the identity of Jesus: he is the messiah, the son of God, the son of man, the teacher and prophet of God. All of the implied Christology of the Gospel of Mark is made explicit through the testimony of Jesus as he stands under the shadow of execution. This drama provides for the reader the key to understanding the central claim of this Gospel: Jesus is indeed the messiah and the son of God (1.1), but this identity can only be understood in the context of service, suffering and death.

At the same time the dramatic confession of 14.62 cannot stand alone. While the trial of Jesus provides the proper context for these titles, the depth and the content of these images must be drawn from the larger story told by this Gospel.

As the reader should know by now, this reciprocal relationship provides the key for reading the Gospel of Mark. Thus the trial scene in Mk 14.53-65 sustains a vital relationship with the larger story of Jesus. Before the religious authorities and in the shadow of the cross the identity of Jesus is made plain. From the beginning of his story (1.1) to its end (14.62), the one condemned to death by the leaders of Israel is messiah and son of God.

The Trial of Peter (Mark 14.66-72)

The story of Peter's denial follows close upon the trial of Jesus. The typical introduction in which the actants are transported to the scene is missing from this account. Because of this the setting for Peter's denial is provided by Mk 15.54, which introduced Peter awkwardly into the scene of the first trial. The opening line (14.66) can thus assume the reader knows where Peter is and why he is there. The implied movement at the end of the scene (14.72c) provides a typical pattern of conclusion.

The scene in Mk 14.66-72 is built around a basic report: Peter's presence at the trial scene is noted; the recognition of Peter as an associate of Jesus is reported; Peter's denial of this claim is asserted; Peter's departure is implied. A modern reader can easily ascertain that the four elements of this basic report are present in all four canonical Gospels. While these elements are consistent, other elements of the story vary from one Gospel to the next. Thus Mk 14.66-72 seems to be rooted in a basic report of Peter's presence outside the trial of Jesus. If this basic account existed, it would serve as an incidental report scene and provide no harsh condemnation of Peter. A reader who steps outside the world of this Gospel would likely identify with Peter; most would lie to escape arrest and possible execution.

It becomes important to note, then, how this story has been presented as an explosive scene of denial. Two internal moves shape the scene. First, the denial has been framed around a temporal device—the cockcrow. The two notices of the cockcrow give to the scene the sense of a ticking timepiece. The story of Peter's denial is extended and intensified by a pattern of threefold repetition. This staging technique creates a retarding pattern and a growing intensity that climaxes in the third denial.

In addition to these internal moves Peter's denial has important external connections. While the cockcrow serves as an internal timepiece, it also connects the story to the prophecy of Mk 14.30, where Jesus predicts Peter's denial. Peter's 'remembering' also points back to the failure predicted in 14.30. The threefold staging of the scene provides exact fulfilment of Jesus' prediction—you will deny me three times (14.30). Most importantly the denial scene has been told in two parts (14.54, 66-72) and used as a frame for the trial of Jesus (14.53, 55-65).

Through these techniques Peter's presence at the trial of Jesus and his attempt to avoid arrest is presented as a scene of dramatic indictment. The connection of Mk 14.54, 66-72 with 14.53, 55-65 invites the reader to see Peter's denial in relation to the trial of Jesus. Witnesses initiate the charge and play a vital role in both accounts. The crucial issue in both stories is the question of identity. In both scenes the response of the accused provides the central focus. Symbolic elements (tearing the garment in 14.63; the cockcrow in 14.68, 72) follow the testimony of the accused.

Through these techniques of narrative linkage and parallel construction Mk 14.53-65 and 14.66-72 are presented as co-temporal mirror images. In the inner scene Jesus is on trial. Outside of the judgment hall Peter is also on trial. The contrast between the two trial scenes is ironic. In the trial of Jesus witnesses testify falsely against him; in the trial of Peter the witnesses speak the truth. The centre of Jesus' trial comes in his dramatic witness to his own identity; the centre of Peter's trial is his threefold denial of his identity as a follower of Jesus. The irony becomes inescapable. Over against false testimony Jesus bears witness to his true identity; over against true witnesses Peter lies about his identity. The ultimate irony emerges in the conclusion of these trial scenes. The lying Peter goes out free and without harm. Jesus, who speaks the truth, is bound and tortured.

In addition to creating interesting reading, this intertwining of the trial of Jesus with the trial of Peter enlarges the scope of each scene. This expansion is most evident in the characterizations that emerge. Seen over against the faithfulness of Jesus the threefold denial by Peter becomes a paradigm of cowardice and abandonment. Seen over against the scene of Peter's denial the portrait of Jesus as the faithful, courageous witness from God is cast in large images across the pages of this narrative.

An alert reader may also see this scene in a much larger context. The denial of Peter is set against the temporal device of the cockcrow. In Mark 13 those who face the traumatic events of the Jewish War and the subsequent coming of the son of man are commanded to be faithful in their witness (13.9-12) and to watch (13.35). The returning master may return at evening or at midnight or early morning. Or the master might return at the cockcrow (13.35). The trial of Peter may thus speak to those who face the trials of the Jewish War and the eschatological woes that will follow—the world of the first reader.

Thus Mk 14.66-72 is told in such a way that the denial scene participates in an intricate series of relationships with the larger Gospel story. These patterns of interconnectedness and reciprocity reshape the significance of this scene and point the reader beyond the world of the story.

The Trial before Pilate (Mark 15.1-15)

The political trial of Jesus is narrated in Mk 15.1-15. This unit has a clear beginning and ending marked off by transition (15.1, 15). In addition the story is framed by the 'handing over' motif: Jesus is handed over to Pilate in 15.1, then handed over to be crucified in 15.15. The question-and-answer format that dominates this scene is similar to the trial of Jesus in 14.53-65 and the trial of Peter in 14.66-72.

The basic pattern of this scene can be seen in the following elements: (1) the gathering of the religious leaders is reported; (2) the political charge is established before Pilate; (3) Jesus is silent in the face of his accusers; (4) the innocence of Jesus is asserted; (5) the death sentence comes into focus; (6) the abuse of Jesus is reported. The alert reader can see numerous connections between this scene and the first trial of Jesus (14.53-65): the three religious groups; the role of the chief priests; the twofold line of questioning addressed to Jesus; a third line of questioning addressed to the people assembled; the silence of Jesus; the innocence of Jesus; the interest in the death sentence; the abuse of Jesus.

Despite these similarities this scene has been developed in a distinct way as a political trial. The nature of the political charge is detailed. Pilate poses the question of sedition (claim to kingship), which presents a capital crime. The ambiguous response of Jesus to the political charge is also noted. Pilate's amazement at the silence of Jesus is described (15.5). The Barabbas incident is reported and linked to the fate of Jesus (15.6-14).

The development of this scene exhibits a concern for the positioning of social groups. Various groups are presented and their role in Jesus' death clarified. Religious leaders, particularly the chief priests, provide the motivation for Jesus' death. A secular authority declares Jesus innocent, but nonetheless provides the means of execution. The crowd operates under the sway of the authorities and demands the death of Jesus. The followers of Jesus are conspicuously absent. Thus the second trial scene is composed with a distinct interest in the polemics and apologetics of social location and identity.

The second trial scene also features a distinct interest in the character-ization of Jesus. The story takes particular care to affirm the innocence of Jesus, to demonstrate his suffering in silence and to note the torture.

Decisive use is made here of threefold patterns. The scene is struc-tured around three separate lines of questioning (15.2, 4-5, 8-14). This pattern invites the reader to connect this story to the first trial, to Peter's trial and to other triadic scenes (Gethsemane, the transfiguration, the three passion predictions). This threefold pattern also creates in Mk 15.1-15 a process of delay and intensification.

As with other triadic scenes the threefold pattern reaches its summit in the third stage. The first line of questioning ends with an ambiguous reply (15.2). The second line of questioning fades away into the silence of Jesus (15.5). This scene reduces the impact of these opening ques-tions and locates the culminative force in the third line of questioning. It is significant that the third line of questioning (15.8-14) centres on the dialogue between Pilate and the people. In this way the story throws the central verdict upon the crowd and the religious leaders who guide them. The silence of Jesus requires that Pilate and the crowd answer each other for their actions. In some sense it is not Jesus but Pilate and the people who are on trial.

This climactic third line of questioning is developed through further use of triads. The third sequence is itself built around three sets of ques-tions to the crowd. In 15.9 Pilate asks if they desire Jesus' release. In 15.12 Pilate asks what he should do with the King of the Jews. The third question (15.14) brings to a climax the exchange between Pilate and the crowd. Thus the third line of questioning reaches its summit in Pilate's third question to the people. This doubly climactic moment is reserved for the ultimate verdict on Jesus: he is innocent.

Following upon this climactic verdict of innocence, the sentence to torture and death (15.15) provides a study in ironic reversal. The hand-ing over to crucifixion in 15.15 is built upon the threefold demand of the crowd (15.13, 14). The reality of the death sentence is established through a single verbal form which is used here for the first time in this Gospel—'crucify'. This pronouncement reverberates with concentric waves of horror and grief: Jesus will die, he will be executed as a crimi-nal, he will be tortured and crucified.

The story of Jesus' political trial has been framed around the Barabbas report (15.6-15a), creating a type of intercalation. As in other intercala-tions in the Gospel of Mark, the inner story interprets the outer scene. Here the intercalation creates a sustained irony. Barabbas, who is guilty of murder (15.7), goes free while Jesus, who is innocent (15.10, 14), is taken away to die. This irony is extended by the name Barabbas, which means 'son of the father'. Barabbas the criminal is freed, but Jesus, the true and innocent son, is sentenced to die.

These various strategies and contours of the trial scene offer up a climactic focus on the identity of Jesus. Amid the frantic verbiage of religious leaders, secular authorities and a frenzied crowd, this story sketches a decisive image of Jesus. This portrait is rooted in the details of the trial scene and framed in the imagery of the Old Testament. In his hour of need Jesus is abandoned by his followers: 'My friends and companions stand aloof from my plague, and my kin stand afar off' (Ps. 38.11). His condemnation by religious authorities recalls 'those who seek my life lay their snares, those who seek my hurt speak of ruin, and meditate treachery all the day long' (Ps. 38.12). He is silent before his accuser 'like a speechless man who does not open his mouth' (Ps. 38.13). His accuser is amazed, recalling the Scripture: 'So shall he startle many nations; kings shall shut their mouths because of him' (Isa. 52.15). He is abused in the place of another as 'one wounded for our transgressions, he was bruised for our iniquities; upon him was the chastisement that made us whole, and with his stripes we are healed' (Isa. 53.5-6). He is sentenced and 'by oppression and judgment he was taken away' (Isa. 53.8). He is condemned to be 'cut off out of the land of the living' (Isa. 53.8). These many connections claim that Jesus is the prophet in whom Israel's Scriptures are fulfilled. In accordance with the Scripture his prophetic mission will reach its summit in his martyrdom.

The Story Thus Far

The four stories in Mk 14.43-15.15 lead up to the death of Jesus. These stories are set in the environs of Jerusalem, and Jesus no longer has control over his movements. From the Mount of Olives he is taken to the quarters of the chief priests, then to Pilate. Step by step the movements of Jesus funnel toward the cross.

While a minimum of action occurs in these scenes, significant advances are made in the plot line. These scenes plot the journey of Jesus to the cross. In doing so various expectations from the previous act (Mk 14.1-42) are realized in the scenes of Mk 14.43-15.15, providing a paradigm of prophecy and fulfilment. Through this process a narrative bridge is constructed between the predictions and symbols of Jesus' death (14.1-42) and the cross event (15.16-16.8). The scenes in Mk 14.43-15.15 put in place the motivation and the means of Jesus' death.

New lines of characterization are also at work in this act. These scenes guide the reader to understand the role of various participants in the death of Jesus. Religious authorities initiate and motivate the death of

Jesus. Secular authorities provide the process of condemnation and the means of death. The crowds that welcomed Jesus into Jerusalem (11.1-11) now act as a persuasive mob that chants for the death of Jesus. The disciples, having fled, are absent. Thus the scenes help the reader to evaluate various groups of actants.

More importantly this act contributes to the characterization of Jesus. The opening scene (Mk 14.43-53a) connects the arrest of Jesus to his teaching in the temple, to the drama in the temple and to the parable of the vineyard. Through these connections the arrest scene provides an important link between prophetic Christology and passion Christology—between the portrait of Jesus as God's prophet and his destiny in Jerusalem.

The first trial (14.53-65) breaks open the messianic secret so persistent through the earlier acts and confirms the status of Jesus: he is messiah, son of God, son of man. The scene of Peter's denial provides a stark contrast to the faithful confession of Jesus. The trial before Pilate (15.1-15) wraps Jesus in the cloak of the Old Testament: he is the righteous and faithful servant who suffers in silence.

This act also completes the characterization of the Twelve. They who have followed Jesus from the Galilee now abandon him in Jerusalem. Their fall is complete: one betrays him, one denies him, all flee. Only in the promise of the resurrection (16.1-8) will they play any further role in this story.

Thus the seventh act of this Gospel prepares the stage for the death of Jesus. This act also prepares the reader. While many Jewish peasants will die cruel and tortured deaths at the hands of the Romans, the reader has been led to understand the unique significance of what is about to happen in Jerusalem.

Mark 15.16–16.8: The Death of Jesus

The eighth and final act of this Gospel extends from Mk 15.16–16.8 and provides the third major unit in the passion account. This unit contains four stories: the abuse and mockery (15.16-20), the crucifixion (15.20c-37), interpretative events (15.38-47) and the resurrection promise (16.1-8).

Abuse and Mockery (Mark 15.16-20)

Notice is given at the end of the trial scene that Jesus is scourged (15.15). Following this report comes a full scene of torture. This scene is carefully delineated from the surrounding events. Three sets of frames operate around the body of this story. (1) Externally the story is framed by the journey to the cross, with specific reference to crucifixion (15.15d, 20c). (2) Jesus is 'led out' at the beginning of the story (15.16), then 'led away' at the end (15.20c). (3) The acts of torture are framed by the changing of clothes. At the beginning of the abuse Jesus is clothed by the soldiers in royal garments (15.17); at the end of the scene he is clothed by the soldiers in his own garments (15.20b).

While this scene has clear boundaries, this is not a self-standing unit; the abuse of Jesus has been woven into the fabric of the trial scene. Various connections to the surrounding material are assumed: Jesus is not be named in the scene, but his identity is clear from the surrounding material; no explanation is needed for the soldiers, who are a logical extension of the political trial; the derision of Jesus as King of the Jews is explained by the previous scene; the procession to crucifixion (15.20c) need not be explained, since it began in the previous story. Because of these connections the scene in Mk 15.16-20 is a carefully developed explication of the abuse reported in both trial scenes.

The triple frame not only delineates the scene; it also focuses the violent action of the inner story. The soldiers are the subject of each deed, with Jesus as the object. In quick succession the soldiers salute, strike, spit, bow, mock. These narrative structures and moves shape the reading of this story. This focused, detailed account moves the reader from the report of abuse (15.15) to a graphic display. Within the reader's world the abuse is transformed from the realm of information to the level of experience.

The abuse scene in Mk 15.16-20 aligns precisely with the political trial

(15.1-15) and serves as its complement. The end of the first trial (14.65) presents the abuse of Jesus within a Jewish ethos: he is condemned by religious authorities, abused by presumably Jewish servants, mocked as a false prophet. In contrast to the religious setting, the abuse of 15.16-20 is rooted in the political trial. Here Jesus is abused by Roman troops, and they taunt him as a pretended king, echoing the charges from the trial (15.2). The reader is to know from these scenes that the death of Jesus has both a religious and a political dimension.

While the scene in Mk 15.16-20 is graphic, it is also anecdotal; it tells what happened, but does little to clarify the significance of these events. Thousands of Jews were abused at the hands of the Romans, and many of them were executed. How is this one any different? The graphic images of 15.16-20 are clarified only when the reader places them in a larger context.

The attentive reader has learned to read reflectively as well as sequentially: stories within stories interpret each other; cycles of repetition are employed; scenes are interpreted by previous accounts. The suffering of Jesus in Mk 15.16-20 is clarified by its relationship with two key themes from the ministry of Jesus: the threefold passion prediction (Mk 8.31; 9.31; 10.32-34) and the parable of the vineyard (Mk 12.1-12).

The passion predictions insert the necessity of suffering into the midst of Jesus' public ministry and redefine his messianic mission. The abuse presented in Mk 14.65, Mk 15.15 and Mk 15.16-20 provides the first realization of this theme. The connection is most precise between Mk 15.16-20 and the third passion prediction (10.32-34). As he predicted, Jesus is handed over to the Gentiles (Mk 10.33). The acts of torture by the Romans match the predictions of Mk 10.34: mocking, striking, spitting, killing. This connection creates a prophecy/fulfilment bond and reminds the reader that suffering is a part of the messianic destiny of Jesus.

The parable of the vineyard also interprets the abuse scene. The religious leaders know that the parable is about them (12.12). Like the efforts of the hired servants, the conspiracy of the leaders is finally successful. Jesus can no longer depart of his own will to safety (12.12), but is here led away to die (15.20c). In this way the prophecy of violence against the son (12.8) is fulfilled in the abuse of Jesus. At the same time the reader is offered an interpretative key to the extraordinary significance of the abuse scene: the abused and silent Jew presented in Mk 15.16-20 is to be understood by the reader as the son—God's chosen, beloved heir.

The attentive reader also knows that the world of this Gospel is framed against the world of the Hebrew Scriptures. The messianic suffering realized in the abuse scene invites the reader to view Jesus in light of

the Suffering Servant hymns (Isa. 42.1-4; 49.1-6; 50.4-11; 52.13-53.12).
Various themes from the Servant Songs are fulfilled in Jesus. He does not
cry or lift up his voice against those who torment him (Isa. 42.2). He
seems to have laboured in vain and to have spent his strength for nothing (Isa. 49.4). Like the Servant of old Jesus has given his back to the
smiters, and he has not hidden his face from shame and spitting (Isa.
50.6). In particular the images of the fourth Servant Song (Isa. 52.13-
53.12) are fulfilled in Jesus:

a marred appearance	Isa. 52.14
despised and rejected	Isa. 53.3
a man of sorrows, acquainted with grief	Isa. 53.3-4
stricken, smitten, afflicted, wounded, bruised	Isa. 53.4-5
oppressed, afflicted	Isa. 53.7
silent in the face of judgment	Isa. 53.7
killed	Isa. 53.8, 9, 12

The scene of mockery is thus informed by a deep heritage of Suffering
Servant images. Drawn from the prophetic traditions of Israel's Scriptures and from the public life of Jesus, these images help the reader to
clarify the events of Mk 15.16-20 and to draw them into the character
sketch of Jesus. At the same time the reader is invited to see that the
concepts of the Suffering Servant and of a servant messiah have been
given concrete reality and definition in the story of Jesus.

The reader has learned another important lesson. While the earlier
scenes offer expectations, as he approaches Jerusalem, that Jesus will be
a king like David (10.35-40, 46-52; 11.1-11), the Christology of kingship
is silenced in the abuse scene. In its place emerges a portrait of Jesus as
the righteous Jewish Servant who suffers and dies in silence.

The Death Scene (Mark 15.20c-37)

The story of Jesus' execution in Mk 15.20c-37 is the most complex unit
in this Gospel. The death scene is built around a simple structural frame:

And they bring him unto the Golgotha place...	22a
And they crucify him...	24a
And with him they crucify two thieves...	27a
But Jesus, having cried out with a great voice, expired.	37

This framework has been filled out with extraordinary colour and detail.

First, this scene is organized around a unique time frame. The death of
Jesus is narrated in three segments, each of which is marked by the passing of three hours. The first segment begins at the third hour (15.25) and
shows the mocking of Jesus. The second segment begins at the sixth
hour (15.33) and is marked by the darkness that covers the land. The

third segment begins at the ninth hour (15.34) and narrates the final throes of death. This temporal device invokes cosmic (solar) images and provides a clear framework for the story.

This scene employs a wider range of actants, many of whom appear for the first (and only) time. Typical characters or groups reappear in this scene: Jesus, religious leaders. Other groups are drawn into the story and used without definition: those who pass by, bystanders, soldiers. Unnamed individuals play vital roles: one offers vinegar, thieves are crucified alongside Jesus. The voice of the narrator, who is also unnamed, surfaces again. New characters are introduced in a way that assumes some level of familiarity on the part of the reader: Simon of Cyrene, Rufus, Alexander. Thus an unusually large and diverse cast of characters inhabits the scene of Jesus' death.

This story also details an extraordinary level of activity around the cross. Some 32 different verbs are used to chronicle the busy scene that surrounds Jesus, yet little attention is given to the actual process of crucifixion.

The narrator is unusually present in this scene. On two occasions narrative commentary translates for the reader the meaning of unfamiliar terms: the name of Golgotha and the cry of Jesus. Beyond this the narrator notes the hour (15.25, 33, 34a) and details the content of the inscription (15.26).

This scene, as is typical of this Gospel, employs various patterns of repetition. Numerous doublets operate here: (1) Jesus is offered something to drink in 15.23 and again in 15.36; (2) the sarcastic call for Jesus to save himself by coming down from the cross is voiced by two different groups (15.30, 31-32b); (3) a loud cry from Jesus is heard in both 15.34 and 15.37.

Several triads operate in the death scene. The crucifixion is announced in 15.20c, in 15.24 and in 15.25. Jesus is mocked by three different groups: passersby in 15.29-30; chief priests in 15.31; those crucified with Jesus in 15.32. As previously noted, the entire scene is divided into three segments marked by three hour spans (15.25, 33, 34a).

Mark 15.20c-37 also contains two patterns of intercalation—a story within a story. At the beginning of the scene the movement of Jesus is separated into his going out (15.20c) and his coming forth (15.22a). Inserted into this opening is the story of Simon. Various details are provided: Simon is from Cyrene, he is coming from the field, he is the father of Alexander and Rufus. The point of this intercalation is simple, but poignant: Simon is conscripted to carry the cross of Jesus.

A second type of intercalation is employed at the end of the death scene. Jesus' 'loud cry' from the cross is reported in both 15.34a and

15.37a. Various images fill the opening between these two reports. Within this interlude bystanders debate the meaning of Jesus' cry. In an echo of Ps. 69.21, someone offers Jesus vinegar. More importantly the interlude is used to interpret the cry of Jesus as the fulfilment of Ps. 22.1. This interlude is also used to address the expectation of Elijah's return (15.35-36).

This scene sets the death of Jesus against the backdrop of the Jewish Scriptures. Scriptural language is employed in numerous places. Psalm 22.18 is quoted in Mk 15.24. The loud cry in 15.34b cites Ps. 22.1, as does its translation. More indirect allusions are also present. The mingled wine (15.23) and the vinegar (15.36) reflect Ps. 69.21. The crucifixion between two thieves echoes Isa. 53.12. The threefold mocking of Jesus suggests several texts from the Old Testament (Pss. 22.7; 109.25; Wis. 2.18). The King of Israel title (15.32) is found in Zeph. 3.15. The darkness that accompanies the loss of a son (15.33) is portrayed in Amos 8.9-10. The expectation of Elijah recalls Mal. 4.5.

How is the death of Jesus different from that of countless other victims of Rome? The death scene is designed to lead the reader to the uniqueness of Jesus' death. For the reader, information about Jesus' death has been transformed into experience. The solar markers and the noonday darkness give this drama cosmic and apocalyptic dimensions. The narrator guides the reader through the narrative, providing information and a sense of companionship. The intercalations fill in the gaps of the story. Doublets and triplets provide emphasis, duration and multiple meanings.

The reader should also take note of what is not present in this scene. Little focus is given to the manner of Jesus' execution, to the physical pain of Jesus or to his emotional state. The death of Jesus is viewed neither from an internal, psychological perspective nor from the omniscient perspective of divinity. The reader, standing alongside countless others, sees from the outside the tragic drama of Jesus' final hours.

The reader of this Gospel has been trained not only to read sequentially, but also to read such stories against the whole range of the Gospel. This reflective reading casts the death of Jesus in a broader light.

In this wider reading the death of Jesus is christologized—it is connected to his identity as the messiah. The only title available to the reader in the death scene is King of the Jews, and this is a misconception. The attentive reader knows, however, the rest of the story. Through the initial passion prediction (8.27-33), Jesus insists that the key to his messianic work is his suffering, death and resurrection. In a similar fashion the mission of the son of man is defined in terms of service and death (10.45). Likewise the Beloved Son is destined to suffering and death (12.1-12). The alert reader sees these images behind the scene of Jesus' death.

The cross is not tied to the destiny of Jesus before Mk 15.13. Prior to this the death of Jesus is foretold, but not in terms of crucifixion. Only through the death scene in 15.20c-37 does the cross become a part of the story of Jesus. Because of this scene the reader can read this destiny back across the full length of Jesus' story.

In a similar way the larger narrative sets the stage for reading this scene. Within this story the role of Simon is almost anecdotal, and no interpretation is added to his deed. But the reader who knows the larger story can already see its significance. Cross-bearing has been defined as a sign of discipleship (Mk 8.34), and the reader is invited to see Simon in this light.

Other important light falls upon this story when it is read against the whole Gospel. The arrogant request to sit in power at the left and right of Jesus (Mk 10.35-40) is cast in an ironic light: those at the left and right of Jesus in the death scene suffer with him in powerlessness. The expectation that Elijah will come to take Jesus from the cross (15.36) is clarified, for Elijah came and died in the form of the Baptist (9.13). The Greek-speaking reader would know that the word for 'breath' and 'Spirit' is the same; thus Jesus' ministry opens with the coming of the Spirit (1.12) and closes with the departure of the Spirit (15.37).

Most importantly reading this scene against the whole of the Gospel clarifies the saving significance of Jesus' death. Read in isolation the events of Mk 15.20c-37 portray the heroic death of a pious, innocent Jew. Through the Passover prophecy (14.22-25), the saving significance of Jesus' death is unveiled. His blood is shed as the source of a new covenant for the many (14.24). His death is a sign of and a step toward the coming Kingdom (14.25). This focus is amplified through the pronouncement of Jesus in Mk 10.45: the son of man has come to serve and to give his life for the many. Only within the larger context of the story of Jesus' life can the reader discover the significance of his death.

Signs of Hope (Mark 15.38-47)

The story told in Mk 15.38-47 is unique in both its form and its function. No introduction or conclusion is employed in this unit. As a result the story is linked directly to the prior death scene and to the subsequent scene at the tomb. At the same time this scene creates an interlude between the death of Jesus and the resurrection report. This interlude imitates the passing of time and undergirds the prophecy that Jesus will be dead for three days (8.31; 9.31; 10.32-34).

This unit is framed around four separate segments with few connections: (1) the rending of the temple veil (15.38); (2) the confession of the centurion (15.39); (3) the experience of the women (15.40-41, 47); (4) the involvement of Joseph of Arimathea (15.42-46). These anecdotal segments present four different experiences in connection with Jesus' death. The narrator is unusually active in this unit, intruding on three occasions (15.40b-41; 15.42; 15.43a, b) to provide vital information. When these segments are joined into a common framework they provide the interpretative keys to the significance of Jesus' death.

The experience of the women has been narrated as two different events, creating a type of intercalation. The women observe the crucifixion in 15.40-41, then observe the place of burial in 15.47. The simple report that the women observe the crucifixion (15.40a) leads to further information on their activity. A specific list of the women witnesses is given (15.40b). A definitive description of their activity is provided (15.41a), including their service to Jesus in the Galilee. Their activity is shown to be indicative of a large group of women who followed Jesus (15.41b). The second report on the women tells that they observed the place of burial (15.47). As with the first report, a precise listing of the witnesses is given.

This report about the women brings startling new information into the last scenes of this Gospel. Typically the Gospel of Mark does not name or describe its characters. This is particularly true of female actants. Prior to Mk 15.40 only the mother of Jesus and Herodias are known by name. Although other women play key roles throughout this story, they are not named. In light of this pattern the naming of the women in Mk 15.40, 47 and in 16.1 is extraordinary. More surprising to the reader, perhaps, is the note that their service at the cross is typical of their lengthy service to Jesus, beginning in the Galilee (15.41). The reader may be even more surprised to learn that there are many such women who follow Jesus (15.41). The role they play is also crucial: they are the only followers of Jesus who remain, and they are the single connection between the death story and the burial of Jesus.

Joseph of Arimathea is introduced for the first time. Precise information about Joseph is provided: he is from Arimathea, a respected citizen, one who awaits the Kingdom of God, one who has courage, one who has access to Pilate.

While these four segments appear almost anecdotal, their role in the telling of Jesus' story is pivotal. In the aftermath of Jesus' death signs of hope emerge.

A divine sign of hope can be seen in the rending of the temple veil. This parting of the veil may be seen as a sign of judgment. If this is the curtain covering the entrance to the Holy of Holies, then its rending desecrates the temple and brings an end to sacrificial worship. The splitting of the veil may also be read as a positive sign: the temple pattern of exclusion by stages of Gentiles, women, disabled people, non-priests has been broken. The barrier that separated individuals from the presence of God is torn asunder with the death of Jesus. The source of this sign is clear. The notation that the curtain is torn from top to bottom (15.38) indicates divine action. The use of the passive form ('it was torn') confirms this as a divine sign of hope that accompanies the death of Jesus.

Hope is also mediated through three human experiences. At the moment of Jesus' death a Roman soldier recognizes him as son of God (15.39). Though all other followers have fled, a few women disciples find the courage to watch from a distance (15.40). A pious Jew finds the courage to ask for Jesus' body, then finds the means for an honourable burial (15.42-46). The place of his burial is known to two named Mary (15.47). The divine sign is accompanied by human experiences that sustain subtle images of hope.

The impact of this interim scene is even more powerful when it is read in light of the entire Gospel story. In this larger context the role of temple worship is clarified. A growing line of hostility is established between Jesus and the temple. Conflict with the religious leadership of Israel is prominent throughout Jesus' Galilean ministry. In Jerusalem this hostility is focused anew as the backdrop for the passion story. Numerous scenes and images set the teaching of Jesus over against the worship life in the temple. This contrast culminates with his prediction that the temple will fall (13.2) The failure of temple worship is signalled anew in Mk 15.38 as the sanctuary is laid open and God's presence is made available to all people.

The reader trained in the ways of this Gospel may learn more about the torn curtain. The term for tearing appears early in the story of Jesus (1.10). The passive verb form in both 1.10 and 15.38 indicate the work of God. Both scenes are followed by a confession that Jesus is God's son (1.11; 15.39). Thus the reader should know that Jesus' entire story and all the scenes of his life are framed by the presence of God.

A similar frame is created around the coming Kingdom. On the first day of his ministry Jesus announces that the Kingdom of God is at hand (1.14-15). On the last day of his life Jesus is buried by one who is expecting the Kingdom of God (15.43).

The larger narrative world also clarifies the confession of the centurion. The confession that Jesus is a son of God may be read as a declaration of Jesus' innocence (Lk. 23.47). The larger flow of this Gospel has made it clear that Jesus is not just a son, but the Beloved Son (1.11; 9.7).

Demons also know this, Peter knows that Jesus is the messiah and Jesus has confessed his identity before the high priest (14.61-62). Consequently the confession in Mk 14.39 is distinct not so much for its content as for its context. Here is the first confession of Jesus as God's son on human lips, and it occurs precisely in the shadow of the cross. The characterization of Jesus, which has been carefully developed and guarded, unfolds at last: here, in view of his suffering and death, Jesus can truly be seen for who he is.

From the larger narrative the reader also learns the significance of what the women have done. In the closing scenes they 'follow' Jesus, they 'serve' him, and they 'watch' with him (14.40, 47). The reader should know by now that in the Gospel of Mark these are terms for discipleship. The anecdotal, retrospective reference to the women in Mk 15.40-41 is thus transformed by the larger narrative into a model of faithful discipleship.

The deeds of Joseph take on new significance in the light of the whole Gospel. Within the larger narrative the actions of Joseph are those expected of a disciple. He awaits the Kingdom whose coming Jesus announced (1.14-15; 15.43). His courage (15.43) demonstrates a trait associated with faith and demanded of disciples (4.40; 6.50). As the followers of the Baptist demonstrate, it is the role of disciples to bury their leader (6.29). Seen in the larger frame of this Gospel, Joseph's heroism provides a model for those who would follow Jesus.

For the first reader, who lives in the aftermath of the fall of Jerusalem, these signs are especially relevant. The death of Jesus does not negate his mission and ministry, but confirms it. The first human to confess Jesus as God's son is a Gentile soldier who does so in the presence of the cross. The burial of Jesus is provided by a respected Jew who awaits the Kingdom of God. The only witnesses and the bearers of this story are women. This interim scene thus generates a new model for the community of faith. This community is not destroyed by the death of Jesus, but rather founded upon this event. This community will be liberated from all the structures that hinder the way to God's presence. Jew and Gentile, male and female alike will participate in the fellowship of this new community. Like the parting of the veil, the life of this community will be the work of God.

For all readers of this Gospel, the interim scene in Mk 15.38-47 means that the story of Jesus is extended beyond his terminal cry. In the Gospel of Mark the execution of Jesus marks the end of his ministry and his last appearance within the world of the story. His final moments are filled with agony and his last words are marked by desperation. The whole story of Jesus is thus stamped with the scandal of his death. Because of this ending the interim scene plays a crucial role. Four signs of hope and a handful of witnesses pave the way to a new beginning at the tomb and in the Galilee.

The Resurrection Promise (Mark 16.1-8)

The text of the Gospel of Mark available to modern readers ended abruptly at 16.8. This has been established through critical analysis of the language and theology of the text and confirmed by the early manu-script tradition.

The scene that closes this Gospel is built around a pattern common to the Gospel of Mark: an opening and closing line of movement frames the central elements of the story (16.1, 8). A simple plot line flows through this unit: the women come to the tomb, there they receive a message, they flee from the tomb in terror. This scene gives unusual attention to detail. Four time markers are used. The women are carefully identified, and clear motivation is provided for their actions. The reader is told what the women experience and how they respond. A detailed description is given of the tomb and the stone. The image of the messenger is described. The narrator intrudes to tell the reader that the stone was very large. This unusual attention to detail lends depth and complexity to this closing scene.

This scene is narrated around a consistent focus on the women. The previous observance of the burial (15.47) makes the scene possible. The story is framed by their movement to and from the tomb. The women are the subject of almost all of the action in the scene. Most importantly the story is told throughout from the viewpoint of the women: the reader sees what they see, hears what they hear, feels what they feel.

While this story is told around the experience of the women, the young man at the tomb provides the centre of the story. The opening movement climaxes not in the finding of the empty tomb, but in the confrontation with the messenger. The movement away from the tomb is a response to his message. Consequently the saying by the young man stands as the centre of this scene.

The impact of this scene upon the larger story and upon the reader is decisive. The tomb scene provides a process of clarification. Many elements and themes from the narrative reach their logical conclusion here. The reader learns here what happened to Jesus. The place, manner and details of Jesus' burial are presented to the reader. The absence of Jesus' body is clarified, and a reappearance in the Galilee is promised.

This scene also clarifies the role of the women. Their actions provide the narrative link between the death of Jesus, his burial and the empty tomb. They provide the sole witnesses in this Gospel to the burial and the empty tomb. Through the activity of the women Peter and the disciples are potentially brought back into the story.

At the same time that this scene is clarifying important events it also sustains a process of narrative suspension. Various elements of the story are left incomplete, and the termination of the plot line means the quest for their significance is suspended. The messenger at the tomb remains enigmatic. Is this an angel? Is this a young human? Is this the first disciple to understand Jesus' destiny? Is this a literary symbol? On these questions the narrative is silent.

The role of the Galilee is uncertain. Will Galilee bring a resurrection appearance? Will the meeting in the Galilee bring instead the eschatological days of Mark 13 and the coming of the son of man? Is Galilee the place of the Gentile mission? Mark 16.1-8 does not say.

The silence of the women creates a dilemma. While others were commanded to silence, then go and tell everyone, the women are commanded to tell, but say nothing. Who, if not the women, will tell the disciples and lead the way to the Galilee? Their silence also silences the voice of the narrative, and Mk 16.1-8 offers no solution for this dilemma. This suspension of signs at the end of the narrative creates a sense of shock and denial, and the readers of this Gospel are not immune from this trauma.

This scene also involves an unusual rupture in the world of the narrative. While the narrator's intrusion (16.4b) provides a type of external voice, the reader is accustomed to this. In contrast to the informative voice of the narrator the mysterious youth at the tomb represents a decisive intrusion. This youth represents the voice of an external witness. Only three such scenes occur in the entirety of this Gospel. At the baptism of Jesus a voice from heaven declares him to be the Beloved Son of God (1.11). On the mount of transfiguration a voice from the cloud again declares Jesus to be God's Beloved Son (9.7). In the door of the empty tomb an external witness provides the final key to Jesus' identity.

Jesus is first identified by the messenger in terms of his human origin: his given name is Jesus and his hometown is Nazareth (16.6). Jesus is then identified as the Crucified One. This is a new title which provides the central image of this scene. The remainder of the message tells the fate of the Crucified One: he has been raised and will go before them into the Galilee. Through this reference to Galilee the messenger gathers the past and the future of Jesus around a central narrative image: he is the Crucified One.

In addition the words of the messenger clarify the task of discipleship. All three external witnesses to Jesus (1.11; 9.7; 16.6) are followed by a call to discipleship: 'follow me' in 1.16-20; 'hear him' in 9.7; 'go to the Galilee' in 16.7. The women are to leave their fear behind (16.6), and they are to go and tell the story about the Crucified One (16.7). This preaching task is to begin with the women and to be carried on by all the followers of Jesus.

This divine mandate is framed and focused through the human experience of lowliness and powerlessness. The promise of Galilee is born in the experience of women whose discipleship is marked by hesitancy, amazement, fear and trembling.

A careful reader should see that this scene brings new light to the larger story of this Gospel. An important frame is built around the passion narrative. This Gospel ends with the story of women who fail to anoint the body of Jesus and with a message shrouded in silence. This disjuncture is given new depth through its connection to the story of Mk 14.1-11. At the beginning of the passion account a woman anoints Jesus for his burial. In contrast to the silence that seizes the women at the tomb, the story of the woman who anointed Jesus will be told, as a part of the gospel message, throughout the world (14.9).

Mark 16.1-8 fulfils the primary line of prophecy in this Gospel. With its promise of resurrection this scene puts into place the final element of Jesus' predictions of his death (8.31; 9.31; 10.32-34).

An important line of characterization develops around the description of Jesus as a Nazarene (16.6). While this description plays a seemingly minor role at other points in the story (1.9; 1.24; 10.47; 14.67), the final use of this title in Mk 16.6 gathers these scattered images into an important line of characterization. The Crucified One who has been raised and will go before the disciples into the Galilee is no figment of spiritual enthusiasm: he bears the concrete history of the Nazarene.

Mark 16.1-8 reverses the command to silence about the identity of Jesus. Demons and those healed and even disciples are silenced during the ministry of Jesus. The transfiguration scene sets the limits of that silence: they are to tell no one until the resurrection of the son of man (9.9). Mark 16.7 thus marks the end of this prohibition and initiates the time of proclamation. The context of this reversal is decisive: true insight and proclamation of Jesus' identity is possible only in relation to his death and resurrection.

The significance of the Galilee is refocused through this scene. The promise of a new experience in the Galilee completes the anti-temple, anti-Jerusalem motif. Over against the failed worship of Jerusalem and its temple, the followers of Jesus are directed to a new future with Jesus in the Galilee. The land of Jesus' past, where the disciples failed so miserably, is thus transformed into a symbol for the future of the church. This connection would prove especially significant for the first reader, who lives in the Galilee in the aftermath of the Jewish War.

The larger narrative brings the witness of the young man into focus. Seen in the reflection of the larger Gospel, the young messenger of 16.5-7 completes a triad of external witnesses. At the beginning of Jesus' story, in the midst of his ministry and now at the end an external voice bears witness to the identity of Jesus and calls for faithful discipleship. This triad reaches a climax in the scene at the tomb.

The attentive reader may see that the entire Gospel has been framed by decisive scenes of presentation and calling (1.1-15; 16.1-8). This places the question of who Jesus is and what it means to follow him as the framework within which to read the entire story.

Consequently Mk 16.1-8 plays a decisive role in the larger flow of this Gospel. The story of Jesus, which has come to an apparent end, is suddenly opened up to the future. Because the plot line is broken off and remains unfinished, the story of Jesus is opened up to the reader of the Gospel and to further developments in the world of the reader. This open-ended text falls into the lap of the reader as a demanding, unfinished story. Within the text reside various options for completing this Gospel: faithful models of discipleship exist alongside tales of cowardice, faithlessness and failure. At the end of this Gospel the reader is left with an unfulfilled command and a gospel not yet proclaimed. Here the final lines of Jesus' identity are put into place: he is the Crucified One who leads the way into God's future. Stark demands are placed on those who would follow Jesus beyond the pages of this story. Disciples are commanded to hear, to follow, to go and tell with courage.

The Story Thus Far

Texts such as the Gospel of Mark can be read in three ways: selectively, sequentially, reflectively. The lectionaries in Christian churches select passages for instruction or preaching, with little attention to the larger contexts of these stories. The Gospel of Mark can also be read sequentially, as one reads a novel. From the text itself the reader has learned that stories from this Gospel must also be read reflectively: the significance of one unit is informed by reflection upon other units. This commentary has worked sequentially through the stories of this Gospel, but always open to sideways glances that might inform individual scenes. At the end of this sequential journey the reader is invited to look back and to reflect upon the whole, for the whole is greater than the sum of its parts. The journey takes on a new perspective for a pilgrim who reaches the goal. The landscape looks different to the climber who attains the summit. So it is with the reader who stands at the end of this Gospel.

Structure

What is the blueprint of this Gospel? How is it constructed and what does it contain? These are the questions of morphology.

The reader can better understand what the Gospel of Mark is by noticing what it is not. The Gospel of Mark is not an oral presentation, so one cannot hear the lilt of the voice, the drip of sarcasm, the groan of desperation, the glimmer of hope. This text is not a visual presentation, so one cannot see the background, observe the scenery, fade in and out or see through the eyes of a character. This Gospel is not a bare historical report that surrounds itself with precise dates and places and witnesses. This Gospel is not a story of the gods, set in the heavens. This Gospel is not a psychological profile of the modern sort. Neither is this story a biography that traces each stage of development and demonstrates influences, causation, introspection.

The Gospel of Mark is a narrative account of Jesus' ministry and death, set in sequential order. This is a selective presentation, for nothing is said of Jesus' birth or childhood. Not every day of his life is narrated. This is also a focused presentation, for some events are highlighted at the expense of others.

This sequential account tells the story of Jesus, so the reader is tempted to see here a biography. But this biography is different from what we know of biographies written under the influence of Greek and Roman culture, and certainly different from modern biographies. To the degree that the story of Jesus is biographical it most resembles a prophetic biography. The telling of Jesus' story is not guided by personal data—date and place of birth, age at death, genealogy, early influences, education—and it exhibits no attempt to catalogue the full sweep of his life. Like the stories of the prophets, Jesus' story is dominated by his vocation—his calling. A prophetic voice opens the story of Jesus (1.1-8). The giving of the call and the response of Jesus open his ministry (1.9-15). Others are invited to take part in this mission (1.16-20). Thus the story of Jesus is told as a sequential account that traces Jesus' obedience to his calling from God.

This narrative is dominated by a coherence of language and style. The story that runs from Mk 1.1 to Mk 16.8 is framed as narrative whole. Various types of stories—genres—are used in the telling of Jesus' life. The most frequent story type is the miracle story. These scenes use a rather standard form that the first readers could recognize: Jesus moves to and from the scene, creating the borders of the unit; a victim or a need is presented; the difficulty of the cure is demonstrated; the healing occurs through a word or a touch; acclamation follows. Another prominent story type is the pronouncement scene. Confronted with a question or a debate, Jesus offers a pronouncement that settles the matter. Numerous parables are used, and the reader is given clues to their interpretation. Various other types of sayings and instructions are collected into this Gospel. A huge block of the Gospel is occupied by the story of Jesus' death (Mk 14-16), creating a passion narrative at the end of the Gospel.

Another important component of this Gospel is the world in which it is told. While the time frame is relative—events in the story are told in relation to other events—the geography is more specific. The major portion of the story of Jesus is told as a journey throughout the Galilee and the surrounding regions. Jesus moves among the villages and synagogues in a world inhabited by peasants, by the sick and the possessed, by tax collectors and sinners, by the curious crowds, by the religious leaders. The second major site of Jesus' story is Jerusalem and its surrounding areas. Here Jesus enters a world dominated by the temple, inhabited by religious leaders, governed by Roman might. The entire Gospel is a Jewish story inhabited by the traditions, suffering, failure, hopes of the people of Israel.

While this Gospel presents a sequential account of Jesus' ministry and death, the reader knows that it does so in episodes—short units with clear borders. This use of episodes within a sequence proves central to the strategy of this Gospel.

Strategy

How does this Gospel present its story? What patterns and connections are established? What strategy is used to present this Gospel to the reader? These are the questions of syntax.

The dynamic of this Gospel is provided by its episodic strategy. The sequential line that flows from the baptism of Jesus to his empty tomb is built upon episodes that focus on selected events in the mission of Jesus. The reader soon learns the layout of such scenes. Most are organic units with rather clear boundaries. Many of these scenes are transportable: they could be found at any number of places in the story. Because of such traits these scenes are interactive: one can shape the telling of another.

The use of such episodes has an important impact on the larger story. First, it breaks the Gospel sequence into manageable units that more easily sustain the interest of the reader. These episodes may also be representative: one story from the synagogue in Capernaum (1.21-38) provides an example of what Jesus does in the synagogues throughout the Galilee (1.39). This episodic strategy also allows the possibility of repetition, cycles, recollection, variation. The work of Jesus in Galilee is told in three major cycles (1.1-3.7a; 3.7-6.6; 6.6b-8.27a) which share a common outline and relate similar episodes. Three passion predictions are given (8.31; 9.31; 10.32-34). This strategy points the reader to important themes that deserve repeating, but also allows nuance and variation upon a familiar pattern. Old stories may be recalled by the reader and seen in a new light. Thus the strategy of using episodes to sustain a sequential narrative brings colour, nuance and dexterity to the telling of Jesus' story.

Other strategic moves may be observed by the reader. In the first place, intentional focus is given to the task of characterization, particularly to the portrait of Jesus. Numerous stories undergo a type of dislocation in which the primary action of a story becomes secondary; it has been replaced by the question of Jesus' identity. Two examples will suffice. In the healing scene of Mk 2.1-12 the reader already knows that Jesus can heal. At the centre of this healing story lie two issues of characterization. 'Who is this who speaks this way?' ask the religious leaders (2.7). Before he heals the wounded man, Jesus answers their question: 'the son of man has authority to forgive sins upon the earth' (2.10). As a corollary to this portrait of Jesus, the religious leaders are also characterized. A second example is found in Mk 14.1-10. In the story of the anointing the woman says nothing. At the centre of this scene stand Jesus' words about his upcoming death and about the spread of the gospel. Thus the spotlight falls not on what she has done, but on what the scene says about Jesus.

The question of Jesus' identity is a strategic priority throughout this Gospel. The issue is introduced in the opening line (1.1), addressed by John the Baptist (1.7-8), declared from heaven (1.11). In the opening day in Capernaum (1.21-28) demons shout and disciples wonder about who Jesus is. This question stands in the midst of Jesus' ministry (8.27-30) and follows him to the cross and the empty tomb. The reader should know that this Gospel gives strategic priority to the characterization of Jesus. Subsequent attention falls upon the character roles of those who seek to follow Jesus and those who oppose him.

A second strategic focus is found in the concern for discipleship. The call to follow Jesus stands at the beginning of his story (1.16-20) and provides the final command at the end (16.7). Through various episodes the reader is offered strategic models in those who seek to follow Jesus. Those expected to succeed fail miserably. Others—mostly unnamed, mostly powerless, mostly women—model in their deeds the demands of faithful discipleship. This strategic focus is aimed not only at those in the story line, but also at the reader of this Gospel (Mk 13.14).

This Gospel also employs a strategy of reciprocity. The reader is invited to interpret one part of the story in the light of other parts. Several scenes are opened up, creating a story within a story, and the reader learns that the stories mutually interpret each other. Other stories are distant, but related. Through various clues the reader is led to understand the prayer in Gethsemane in connection with the predictions of Mark 13. Such a reading strategy realigns both units. The agony of prayer and the failure to watch are placed in an ultimate context; the catastrophes of Mark 13 begin to unfold in the story of Gethsemane. The Gospel itself is to be read in the light of reciprocity. Jesus' ministry is marked by scenes of wonder, power, expectation, while the story of his death is scandalous. Prophetic Christology and passion Christology collide in this Gospel, and it is only the strategy of reciprocity that guides the reader through this impact. The one crucified in Jerusalem is none other than Jesus, the Galilean teacher from Nazareth (16.6). The greatest achievement of this Gospel is its ability to link the suffering and death of Jesus to his wondrous ministry of word and deed.

It is this strategy of reciprocity that offers the reader a coherent account of Jesus, both within the story and beyond. His messianic mission leads to this death. The meaning of Jesus' death is rooted in the stories of his ministry. The one who goes before the disciples into the future is none other than Jesus, the crucified Nazarene. Through this strategy the life of Jesus in the Galilee, his death in Jerusalem and his future as the son of man are linked.

Significance

What is the point of all of this? What is this Gospel saying? How does it see the world? What are its values and claims and demands? What are the signs created by this Gospel and presented to the reader? These are questions of significance and signification.

The Gospel of Mark offers a complex of signs and signification, but five are central to the identity of this Gospel. The sign that frames the whole of this Gospel is the coming of the Kingdom of God. In the Gospel of Mark the first words of Jesus announce the nearness of God's Reign (1.14-15). The parables contain the mystery of the Kingdom (4.10-11). The children who come to Jesus are a sign of the Kingdom (10.13-16), but the rich will find it difficult to enter the Kingdom (10.24). A scribe who heeds the Scriptures of Israel is not far from the Kingdom of God (12.34). Jesus' last meal with his disciples points to the new day when he will drink anew with them in the Kingdom (14.25). He is buried by one who awaits the Kingdom (15.43). Thus the story of Jesus is framed and permeated with the expectation of God's Reign. Because this concept frames the larger story, the episodes that unfold within this frame may be seen as explication of that theme: in the words and deeds, the suffering and death of Jesus, the Reign of God has drawn near. The sign of the coming Kingdom is placed over the entirety of the Gospel story.

The second major sign is found in its portrait of Jesus. This Gospel insists that the Kingdom comes precisely in the ministry of Jesus. While the Gospel is framed by the sign of the Kingdom, its most pervasive focus is the identity of Jesus. In the opening lines he is named, for the reader, as the messiah and the son of God (1.1). The miracle stories, pronouncements, parables, controversies and titles contribute to his image. A strong prophetic characterisation emerges from the ministry of Jesus: he is the wondrous teacher whose words and deeds demonstrate the power of God's Kingdom. Passion predictions dominate the latter part of his ministry (8.31; 9.31; 10.32-34), and in the environs of Jerusalem a strong passion Christology develops. The text helps the reader to negotiate these images into a coherent portrait of Jesus. The central question is found on the lips of Jesus in Mk 8.29: 'But who do you say that I am?' The multiple answers offered to the reader provide the primary significance of this Gospel.

The Gospel of Mark insists not only *that* the Kingdom is near in Jesus; it also traces the impact of its arrival. In the Gospel of Mark the Kingdom is a movement of liberation and its arrival is marked by the crossing of boundaries. This is the third major sign of this Gospel. The miracles of Jesus are not displays of magic: they are powerful signs of the arrival of God's Reign. In the wonders of Mk 1.21-3.7a various boundaries that separate humans from God are crossed: evil spirits, disease, uncleanness, sin, oppressive religious traditions and structures. In the second act (Mk 3.7-6.6) the crossing of boundaries continues. The call to the Kingdom is extended to women and to foreigners. A new understanding of insiders and outsiders is established. The kingdom of Satan is invaded. Jesus travels to the Gerasenes, who live on the 'other side'. The line separating Jew from Gentile is breached. A dead daughter is brought to life, and a wounded daughter is released unto faith, salvation, wholeness, peace. The third act (6.6b-8.27a) continues this assault on the boundaries. The law is interpreted as a guide for humans rather than as a ritual or a legalistic code. The boundary excluding women and Gentiles is brought down. A new community of God's people is gathered, and Gentiles are among this community. The fourth act (8.27-10.52) confirms a developing theme: the most difficult boundary of all is found in the blindness, misunderstanding, cowardice and greed that prevent true discipleship. As the healing of Bartimaeus (10.46-52) shows, true discipleship is the greatest miracle of all.

Jesus confronts a different set of boundaries in the Jerusalem scenes: the temple establishment, the religious leaders, the fall of Jerusalem, the end of the age, the end of his own life. How can the story of Jesus survive these catastrophes? How can his followers move past these events? Key signs are given to the alert reader. The fall of Jerusalem and the destruction of the temple are not the end of the world (Mk 13). In the aftermath of their fall discipleship will endure and the gospel will be spread to all nations. The keepers of Israel's vineyard will be judged (Mk 12.1-12), and a new community of faith will arise in the aftermath of the temple. After Jesus is struck down, he will be raised up to lead his disciples into Galilee (14.27-28; 16.6-7). The narrative surrounds these events with signs of hope. The two most potent of these are the torn veil and the empty tomb. The rending of the temple veil (15.38) signals, at the moment of Jesus' death, that the temple has fallen and the presence of God has been made available to all people. The empty tomb (16.1-8) signals that the death of Jesus was not the end of his story, nor that of his followers.

Through these episodes in the Galilee and in Jerusalem a clear sign is given. The Kingdom of God that stands near in Jesus is a movement of liberation: it will overcome every barrier that separates humans from the saving presence of God.

In connection with the liberating advance of the Kingdom, a fourth major sign is built around the religious leadership of Israel. Though there are some exceptions, religious leaders in the Gospel of Mark are shown to fail God and abandon Israel. They engage in debate and controversy with Jesus, then they plot his death. They are more concerned for Sabbath rules than for human need. They have allowed the temple to become a place of commerce that robs widows. They are aligned with the political barons of Jerusalem. They plot the death of Jesus, arrange his arrest, pervert justice at his trial, hand him over to the government, demand his crucifixion, revile his suffering. While this sign may seem at times disproportionate and stereotypical, the condemnation of the leaders of Israel is built on a prophetic model and precedent. In addition the primary audience of this sign stands not in the day of Jesus, but in the aftermath of the first Jewish War, when a new beginning is not only desired, but absolutely necessary.

This sign is directed precisely against the temple. The temple has become a place of thieves which takes the last coins of widows. The teaching of Jesus is rejected there, and its leaders take part in his death. In the prophecy of Jesus the temple's destruction is assured, and a new beginning is demanded. This message is uniquely relevant for the reader who, in the aftermath of the temple's fall, seeks a new direction for faith in God.

The last major sign is one that endures far beyond the range of this Gospel: the difficulty of what it means to follow Jesus. The failure of the disciples is played out in painful detail in the scenes of this Gospel. Beginning in the Galilee the disciples fail to understand Jesus, they grow cowardly and impotent and they are overcome by self-interest. The concept of discipleship as a way of suffering and service and death lies beyond their grasp. In Jerusalem the dangers of failure are realized. Despite their boasts of fidelity and courage, one betrays Jesus, one denies him, all flee, one flees naked. None of the Twelve are to be found at the scene of the cross or at the empty tomb. In the end even the faithful women flee with fear and trembling and say nothing to anyone. If discipleship is to endure beyond the tragic events of Jerusalem, it will take a miracle. The reader is offered this sign as a guide and warning for all who seek to follow Jesus.

While significance abounds in this story, the world of this Gospel is dominated by a constellation of five major signs. These signs present the value system of this Gospel—its message, its world-view, its demands. These signs are more than information—they are at once claim and warning. These signs are wrapped in the images of human history, they are sketched in the contours of the text and they are aimed at the reader.

Like the notations on the edge of ancient maps, these signs provide both
warning and invitation.

Meaning

What does this mean? How is the reader to appropriate and apply what
is written here? In order to address this question, several distinctions are
necessary. First, the reader must be able to distinguish between history
and story. History is a record of facts; a story is a selected telling which
may use history. Stories do not tell all the facts, but select those that
matter most and place them in a particular spotlight. Thus the Gospel of
Mark does not give Jesus' hat size, which would certainly be a historical
fact, but it does tell about the power of his teaching. The Gospel of Mark
is story; it is built upon history, but its story is much more important
than the facts. This story is, by its own description, a Gospel; it claims to
show the saving significance of God's work in Jesus. The form and the
content of the Gospel of Mark suggest a kerygmatic (preaching) function
that holds priority over all others. The entire work is a message about
Jesus (1.1). The central task of Jesus is proclamation (1.14-16, 22-23, 39).
Disciples are to go and tell what they have seen and heard (3.13-14;
5.20; 6.7-13; 13.10; 14.9; 16.7). The reader must know what is being
read.

The reader must also be able to distinguish between the elements of a
story and the signs they create. The Gospel of Mark tells of Jesus' miracles, but other texts tell of miracles by other people. What is significant
about these stories in the Gospel of Mark is not that Jesus does miracles,
but that his miracles are a sign of the coming Kingdom. The release and
healing demonstrated in the miracle stories is not magic, but liberation.
The salvation at work in these scenes is the sign offered to the reader.

The reader must also learn to distinguish significance from meaning.
Significance resides in a text; it is created by the interaction of narrative
elements and strategies. The Gospel of Mark signifies, for example, that
Jesus is the Son of God. Even when the text is closed and the reader is
absent, these literary signs are still present. Signification is the work of
the text. Meaning is something altogether different. A text has meaning
only when a reader takes up that text and appropriates it in some way.
Closed texts have significance, but no meaning. Meaning is negotiated in
the interaction of the reader with the text. The text brings its signals and
its biases to this dance, but so does the reader. The reader may reject the
significance of the text or the reader may interpret in a way that is not
appropriate to the text. What the text means also depends upon the skill
and the world-view and the motivations of the reader. Thus texts may

mean different things to different readers, and a text may mean different things to the same reader in a different context or time.

So we cannot ask what the text means for all time, to all readers. We can only ask how certain readers would understand this text and how faithful their reading is to the signs of the text. Even here, we can only speak in general terms and with great reservation, for the possibilities of meaning are many. Having sought the significance of this Gospel, we turn now to what it might mean to the first reader, then to a modern reader.

The Gospel of Mark and the First Reader

Most scholars place the writing of this Gospel somewhere in the years surrounding the first Jewish War (66-74 CE). While some form of the text was likely in production earlier, the Gospel as we have it reflects an awareness of what is happening to Jerusalem in the 70s. Thus multiple levels of communication are at work here. While the story speaks of events that occurred in the late 20s, it addresses an audience some 40 years after these events. The first reader likely lives in a Galilean community of faith in the aftermath of the fall of Jerusalem and the temple. All of Judaism is in disarray, including that portion which follows Jesus as the messiah. The community of the Essenes was destroyed in 68 CE. With the fall of the temple, the Sadduccees and the scribes, the elders and the Sanhedrin lose their power. A vacuum is created by the fall of the temple, the dissolution of traditional religious authority and the flight from Jerusalem. Has God abandoned Israel? Where does faith go from here?

Numerous new models arise, most prominent among them the work of the Pharisees in the synagogues of Palestine and Syria and beyond. Another significant movement is also afoot in the aftermath of the temple. There are communities of faith which maintain their connection to the story of Israel, but do so through faith in Jesus as God's messiah. Among these scattered communities of believers are one or more in the Galilee. While missionaries such as Paul build their gospel solely on the death and resurrection of Jesus, communities such as this one know the story of his life. These stories survive in their worship and in their work, and they struggle to understand how the wonder of Jesus' life fits with the scandal of his death. The outcome of this tradition working in the life of a community over many years is a written, narrative account of the life and death of Jesus. This is the Gospel of Mark, and it falls into the hands of the first reader as a Gospel—the story of God's salvation in Jesus the messiah.

When the first reader takes up this text and grasps the signs of this

Gospel, what does it mean in the Galilee in the aftermath of the Jewish War? First, the Gospel of Mark clarifies the landscape of the Galilee in the 70s. As Jesus predicted (Mk 13), catastrophe has come, but the world has not ended. The temple is gone, but faith survives. Political powers and persecution have encircled believers, but they endure. The end is not yet. There is work to be done. With endurance and watchfulness, they are to take the gospel beyond the boundaries of Israel to all the nations. The failure of the temple and its supporters is no accident of history, but rather the fulfilment of a prophecy rooted in the disobedience of Israel. This does not mark the end of Israel's story, but a new beginning. Not only the temple, but also the disciples of Jesus have failed. The Gospel of Mark declares that a new beginning is also possible with the followers of Jesus.

This story also means, for the first reader, that the death of Jesus in Jerusalem was not the final word. His death opened a new way and a new vision. He himself promised to lead his followers into that new future. Those who choose to remain faithful should look beyond Jerusalem to the new work in the Galilee.

How should the first reader live in the Galilee of this new time and place? The answer is to be found in the old story of Galilee. The Galilee is the place where Jesus announced the coming of the Kingdom, the place where he healed and preached and taught. Galilee is the place of controversy and debate, of calling and struggle in the way of discipleship. Galilee is the place of the Gospel. Thus the first reader may hear at the end of the Gospel of Mark a personal call to return to the Galilee (16.7) and there, in the presence of the Risen One, to continue the work.

What does the gospel look like in the new Galilee? For the first reader the gospel of God (1.14) can never be bound to structures (such as the temple) or to traditions (washing hands, fasting, sacred times and places) or to legal codes. For the first reader the story of Jesus means the gospel will break down every barrier that separates people from the full life of God's salvation. The tumbled walls of a ruined temple cannot bind the gospel. The military might of Rome cannot stop its advance. Even stubborn leaders and blind disciples can be overcome. There is nothing in the world of the first reader—social, religious, political—that the gospel of God will not break down and pass through in its movement of human liberation. The gospel is bound for the ends of the earth (13.10; 14.9), and the desperate Galilee of the first reader can also be a part of the gospel story.

What does the new community of faith look like? It consists not of structures and rituals and rules, but of a movement of liberation. Jews and Gentiles take part together, the poor and wounded and outcast are welcomed, the presence of God is available to all. Built on faith and prayer and the work of the gospel, this community is guided by the teachings of Jesus and sustained by the shepherding power of God.

The Gospel of Mark and Modern Readers

Modern readers do not live in the Galilee—neither the Galilee of Jesus nor the Galilee of the first reader. Can this text mean anything to a modern reader? The image of God drawn in this story suggests it can.

The Gospel of Mark signifies, in agreement with the Hebrew Scriptures, that the heart of religion is found in the twofold command: love God, love your neighbour. In an age where religion is big business and prime time entertainment, when religion exerts control over governments and industries and armies, the religion of Jesus means radical reform. The religion of Jesus means that love of God cannot be reduced to personal religious experience, but always has an ethical dimension. The religion of Jesus means that true goodness has its roots in Godliness. The religion of Jesus means that in this age, faith and ethics are irrevocably linked.

Jesus' view of power means that, even in the modern world, power is not what it seems to be. Political authority is not final, and it is not lasting. Institutional structures can and do fall. Control should not be misunderstood as authority. Sometimes truth is found among the simple, and sometimes the weak and excluded are the most powerful of all.

Can the individual teachings of Jesus mean anything in our world? If that means embracing the world-view of Jesus—a flat earth, inhabited by demons, soon to end—then probably not. Again the reader must learn to distinguish story from significance. If demons can be driven out in this Gospel, a modern reader does not have to embrace the world of the story to embrace the significance of these scenes. The principles that emerge from Jesus' teaching can indeed be meaningful to the modern reader. The teaching of Jesus means that humans are more important that institutions and traditions—even religious institutions and traditions. The teaching of Jesus means that service, not dominance, still counts for greatness. Jesus' teachings mean that God is still at work in the world and that human integrity and courage and community are still possible.

The boundary-crossing motif of this Gospel proves especially meaningful in the world of the modern reader. If salvation is related to health and wholeness in the spiritual and social and physical realms of human life (as it is in the Gospel of Mark), then the gospel is a powerful force for liberation. In the world of the modern reader this text declares that

God is on the side of human healing and wholeness and stands over against all boundaries and strictures that separate humans from this life. Spiritual blindness, hunger, poverty, AIDS, war, racism, ethnic cleansing, nationalism, militarism—the call to the Kingdom demands their end. The Gospel of Mark insists that Jesus' call requires our participation in this mission. In the world of the modern reader, as in the world of the first reader, this liberation and salvation can only happen through prayer that is empowered in service, suffering, courage, faithfulness, endurance.

The Gospel of Mark demands of the modern reader a new community. This community will be centred in faith, open to all, committed to service.

The power of this Gospel to create from the story of Jesus signs that speak to modern readers is modelled in two scenes. In Mk 1.40-45 Jesus is confronted by a leper. This leper suffers from a physical disease, but also from religious sanction and social shunning. The leper is an untouchable, fenced off from God and the human community. The power of the Kingdom that Jesus proclaims is demonstrated in this story in Jesus' deeds. Through the act of touching Jesus brings the leper back into the human community and declares this victim to be ritually and socially clean. His healing provides a clear sign: it demonstrates and proclaims the reality of God's Reign, but it also highlights the failure of the religious establishment. In the world of the modern reader the sign of the leper offers meaning for the suffering of AIDS victims. Beyond their physical assault, HIV carriers are fenced off from normal human discourse and subject to religious sanction. If the gospel of the Kingdom is about liberation from leprosy in the world of Jesus, then it is about liberation from AIDS in the world of the modern reader.

The healing of Bartimaeus in Mk 10.46-52 also models the significance— the sign making—of this Gospel. A bothersome beggar demands the healing touch of Jesus, then uses his sight to follow Jesus in the way of discipleship. He has done what the Twelve, through blindness and obstinence and cowardice, have failed to do. Whereas they asked for power and honour from Jesus, Bartimaeus asks for sight and discipleship. He is a sign, within the world of this Gospel, that true discipleship is a miracle. Such obedience is found only in the path of suffering and service, and it is often found among those cast by the wayside. The power of this sign endures, and it proves no less insistent in the world of the modern reader.

Thus the Gospel of Mark falls into the lap of the modern reader as a text filled with significance and with potential meaning. Love of God and love of neighbour provide the heart of true religion. In the coming of God's Reign every boundary separating humans from salvation—from full relationship with God and with the human community—is brought under siege. This is the story underway in the Gospel of Mark. Having discerned the ways of this Gospel and learned to read its signs, the modern reader is invited to complete the story. What happens next? Where does the story go from here? Only the reader knows.

Epilogue

Albert Schweitzer (1875-1965) held three doctorates: in theology, in philosophy and in medicine. In addition he was an accomplished organist; he rebuilt many of the great organs of Europe and he was an expert on the works of Johann Sebastian Bach. At age 38, at the height of his career, Schweitzer left behind the academic life of Europe. He established a hospital in equatorial Africa along the banks of the Ogowe river in a village called Lambarene. He used the income from his Nobel Peace Prize to expand the hospital and to construct a colony for lepers. He spent the bulk of his life in Lambarene, seeking to live out the gospel of Jesus among the poor and sick. When asked to place his extraordinary sacrifice and discipleship in the perspective of modern humanity, Schweitzer offered these words: 'Every man has his Lambarene.' So it is with the Gospel of Mark, from the disciples in the story to the first reader to modern readers: everyone has a Galilee.

Bibliography

Achtemeier, P.J., *Invitation to Mark* (Garden City, NY: Image Books, 1978).
—*Mark* (Proclamation Commentaries; Philadelphia: Fortress Press, 1975).
Anderson, H., *The Gospel of Mark* (NCB; London: Marshall, Morgan & Scott, 1976).
Auerbach, E., Mimesis: *The Representation of Reality in Western Literature* (trans.
    W. Trask; Princeton, NJ: Princeton University Press, 1953 [1946]).
Beardslee, W., *Literary Criticism of the New Testament* (Philadelphia: Fortress Press,
    1970).
Belo, F., *A Materialist Reading of the Gospel of Mark* (Maryknoll, NY; Orbis Books,
    1981).
Best, E. 'The Miracles in Mark', *RevExp* 75 (1978), pp. 539-54.
—*The Temptation and the Passion: The Markan Soteriology* (Cambridge: Cam-
    bridge University Press, 1965).
Bieler, L., *ΘΕΙΟΣ ΑΝΗΡ: Das Bild des 'Göttlichen Menschen' in Spätantike und
    Frühchristentum* (Darmstadt: Wissenschaftliche Buchgesellschaft, 1967).
Black, C., *The Disciples according to Mark: Markan Redaction in Current Debate*
    (Sheffield: JSOT Press, 1989).
Blevins, J., *The Messianic Secret in Markan Research, 1901-1976* (Washington:
    University of America Press, 1981).
Boobyer, G., 'Galilee and Galileans in St Mark's Gospel', *BJRL* 35 (1953), pp. 334-48.
Branscomb, B.H., *The Gospel of Mark* (MNTC; London: Hodder & Stoughton, 1952).
Broadhead, E.K., 'Mark 1, 44: The Witness of the Leper', *ZNW* 83 (1992), pp. 257-65.
—*Naming Jesus: Titular Christology in the Gospel of Mark* (JSNTSup, 175; Sheffield:
    Sheffield Academic Press, 1999).
—*Prophet, Son, Messiah: Narrative Form and Function in Mark 14-16* (JSNTSup,
    97; Sheffield: JSOT Press, 1994).
—*Teaching with Authority: Miracles and Christology in the Gospel of Mark*
    (JSNTSup, 74; Sheffield: JSOT Press, 1992).
—'Which Mountain is "This Mountain"? A Critical Note on Mark 11.22-25', *Paradigms*
    2 (1986), pp. 33-38.
Bultmann, R., *The History of the Synoptic Tradition* (trans. J. Marsh; New York:
    Harper & Row, rev. edn, 1963 [1921]).
—*Theology of the New Testament* (trans. K. Grobel; New York: Charles Scribner's
    Sons, 1951 [1948]).
Burkhill, T.A., *Mysterious Revelation: An Examination of the Philosophy of St
    Mark's Gospel* (Ithaca, NY: Cornell University Press, 1963).
Carrington, P., *According to Mark* (Cambridge: Cambridge University Press, 1960).
Chatman, S., *Story and Discourse* (Ithaca, NY: Cornell University Press, 1978).
Chomsky, N., *Aspects of the Theory of Syntax* (Cambridge, MA: MIT Press, 1965).
—*Syntactic Structures* (The Hague: Mouton, 1957).
Cranfield, C.E.B., *The Gospel according to St Mark* (CGTC: Cambridge: Cambridge
    University Press, 1959).
Culler, J., *Structuralist Poetics* (Ithaca, NY: Cornell University Press, 1975).

Culpepper, R.A., *Anatomy of the Fourth Gospel* (Philadelphia: Fortress Press, 1983).
—'The Passion and the Resurrection in Mark', *RevExp* 74/4 (1978), pp. 583-600.
Dewey, K., 'Peter's Curse and Cursed Peter', in Kelber (ed.), *The Passion in Mark*, pp. 96-114.
Dibelius, M., *From Tradition to Gospel* (trans. B.L. Woolf; Cambridge: James Clarke, 1971 [1919]).
—*Gospel Criticism and Christology* (London: Ivor, Nicholson & Watson, 1935).
Donahue, John R., *Are You the Christ? The Trial Narrative in the Gospel of Mark* (SBLDS, 10; Missoula, MT: University of Montana Press, 1973).
—'Temple, Trial, and Royal Christology', in Kelber (ed.), *The Passion in Mark*, pp. 61-79.
Dormeyer, D., *Die Passion Jesu als Verhaltensmodell: Literische und theologische Analyse der Traditions- und Redaktionsgeschichte der Markuspassion* (Münster: Aschendorff, 1974).
Dschulnigg, P., *Sprache, Redaktion und Intention des Markus-Evangeliums: Eigentümlichkeiten der Sprache des Markus-Evangeliums und ihre Bedeutung für die Redaktionskritik* (SBB; Stuttgart: Katholisches Bibelwerk, 1986).
Eagleton, T., *Literary Theory* (Minneapolis: University of Minnesota Press, 1983).
Evans, C.F., 'I will go before you into Galilee', *JTS* 5 (1954), pp. 3-18.
Fowler, R., *Loaves and Fishes: The Function of the Feeding Stories in the Gospel of Mark* (SBLDS; Chico, CA; Scholars Press, 1981).
Frye, N., *Anatomy of Criticism* (Princeton, NJ; Princeton University Press, 1957).
Fuller, R.H., *Interpreting the Miracles* (Philadelphia: Westminster Press, 1963).
Funk, R., 'The Form of the New Testament Healing Miracle Story', *Semeia* 12 (1978), pp. 57-96.
Genette, G., *Narrative Discourse: An Essay in Method* (trans. J.E. Lewin; Ithaca, NY: Cornell University Press, 1980).
Geulich, R., *Mark 1-8.26* (WBC; Dallas: Word Books, 1989).
—'The Gospel Genre', in P. Stuhlmacher (ed.), *Das Evangelium und die Evangelien* (Tübingen: J.C.B. Mohr, 1983).
Gnilka, J., *Das Evangelium nach Markus* (EKKNT; Zürich: Benzinger Verlag, 1978).
Gould, E., *The Gospel according to St Mark* (New York: Charles Scribner's Sons, 1896).
Grundmann, W., *Das Evangelium nach Markus* (THKNT; Berlin: Evangelische Verlagsanstalt, 6th edn, 1973).
Gundry, R., *Mark: A Commentary on his Apology for the Cross* (Grand Rapids: Eerdmans, 1993).
Güttgemanns, E., *Candid Questions concerning Gospel Form Criticism* (trans. W. Dotey; Pittsburgh: Pickwick Press, 1979).
Hahn, F., *The Titles of Jesus in Christology* (trans. H. Knight and G. Ogg; London: Lutterworth, 1969).
Hengel, M., *Studies in the Gospel of Mark* (trans. J. Bowden; London: SCM Press, 1985).
Hooker, Morna, *The Gospel according to St. Mark* (London: A. & C. Black, 1991).
—*The Son of Man in Mark* (London: SPCK, 1967).
Iersel, B. van, *Mark: A Reader-Response Commentary* (trans. W.H. Bisscheroux; Sheffield: JSNTSup, 164; Sheffield Academic Press, 1998).
Jeremias, J., 'Die Salbungsgeschichte Mc 14, 3-9', *ZNW* 35 (1936), pp. 77-81.
Juel, D., *Messiah and Temple: The Trial of Jesus in the Gospel of Mark* (SBLDS; Missoula, MT: Scholars Press, 1977).

Karnetzki, M., 'Die galiläaische Redaktion im Markusevangelium', *ZNW* 52 (1961), pp. 238-72.

Keck, L., 'Mark 3.7-12 and Mark's Christology', *JBL* 84 (1965), pp. 341-58.

Kee, H.C., *Community of the New Age: Studies in Mark's Gospel* (Philadelphia: Westsminster Press, 1977).

Kelber, W.H., 'From Passion Narrative to Gospel', in *idem* (ed.), *The Passion in Mark: Studies in Mark 14-16* (Philadelphia: Fortress Press, 1976), pp. 153-80.

—'The Hour of the Son of Man and the Temptation of the Disciples', in *idem* (ed.), *The Passion in Mark*, pp. 41-60.

—*The Kingdom in Mark: A New Place and a New Time* (Philadelphia: Fortress Press, 1974).

—'Mark 14.32-42: Gethsamene', *ZNW* 63 (1972), pp. 166-87.

—*Mark's Story of Jesus* (Philadelphia: Fortress Press, 1979).

—*The Oral and the Written Gospel: The Hermeneutics of Speaking and Writing in the Synoptic Tradition, Mark, Paul, and Q* (Philadelphia: Fortress Press, 1983).

Kermode, F., *The Genesis of Secrecy* (Cambridge, MA; Harvard University Press, 1979).

Kertelge, K., Die *Wunder Jesu im Markusevangelium: Eine redaktionsgeschichtliche Untersuchung* (SANT; Munich: Kösel, 1970).

Kingsbury, J.D., *The Christology of Mark's Gospel* (Philadelphia: Fortress Press, 1983).

—*Conflict in Mark: Jesus, Authorities, Disciples* (Minneapolis: Fortress Press, 1989).

Klostermann, E., *Das Markusevangelium* (HNT; Tübingen: J.C.B. Mohr, 1950).

Koch, D.-A., *Die Bedeutung der Wundererzählungen für die Christologie des Markusevangeliums* (Berlin: W. de Gruyter, 1975).

Kuhn, H.-W., *Ältere Sammlungen im Markusevangelium* (Göttingen: Vandenhoeck & Ruprecht, 1971).

Lane, W., 'From Historian to Theologian: Milestones in Markan Scholarship', *RevExp* 75 (1978), pp. 601-17.

—*The Gospel according to Mark: The English Text with Introduction, Exposition and Notes* (NICNT: Grand Rapids: Eerdmans, 1974).

Lentriccha, F., *After the New Criticism* (Chicago: University of Chicago Press, 1980).

Lepschy, G.C., *A Survey of Structural Linguistics* (London: André Deutsch, 1982).

Lohmeyer, E., *Das Evangelium nach Markus* (Göttingen: Vandenhoeck & Ruprecht, 10th edn, 1937).

—*Galiläa und Jerusalem* (Gottingen: Vandenhoeck & Ruprecht, 1936).

Luz, U., 'Das Geheimnismotiv und die Markinische Christologie', *ZNW* 56 (1965), pp. 9-30.

—'Theologica Crucis al Mitte der Theologie im NT', *EvT* 34 (1974), pp. 131-39.

Mack, Burton, *Mark and Christian Origins: A Myth of Innocence* (Philadelphia: Fortress Press, 1988).

Malbon, E.S., *Narrative Space and Mythic Meaning in Mark* (New Voices in Biblical Studies; San Francisco: Harper & Row, 1986).

Marin, L., *Semiotik der Passionsgeschichte: Die Zeichensprache der Ortsangaben und Personennamen* (trans. S. Virgils; Munich: Chr. Kaiser Verlag, 1976).

Martin, R., *Mark: Evangelist and Theologian* (Grand Rapids: Zondervan, 1972).

Marxsen, W., *The Beginnings of Christology, together with the Lord's Supper as a Christological Problem* (trans. P. Achtemeier and L. Nieting; Philadelphia: Fortress Press, 1979 [1960]).

—*Mark the Evangelist: Studies on the Redaction History of the Gospel* (trans. J. Boyce, D. Juel and W. Poehlmann; Nashville: Abingdon Press, 1969).

McKnight, E.V., *Meaning in Texts: The Historical Shaping of a Narrative Hermeneutics* (Philadelphia: Fortress Press, 1978).

Neirynck, F., *Duality in Mark: Contributions to the Study of the Markan Redaction* (Leuven: Leuven University Press, 1972).

Nineham, D.E., *The Gospel of St Mark* (Baltimore: Penguin Books, 1963).

Perrin, N., *A Modern Pilgrimage in New Testament Christology* (Philadelphia: Fortress Press, 1974).

Pesch, R., *Das Markusevangelium* (HTKNT; Freiburg: Herder, 3rd edn, 1980).

Petersen, N., *Literary Criticism for New Testament Critics* (Philadelphia: Fortress Press, 1978).

Polhill, J., 'Perspectives on the Miracle Stories', *RevExp* 74 (1977), pp. 389-99.

Pryke, E.J., *Redactional Style in the Marcan Gospel: A Study of Syntax and Vocabulary as Guides to Redaction in Mark* (London: Cambridge University Press, 1978).

Quesnell, Q., *The Mind of Mark: Interpretation and Method through the Exegesis of Mark 6.52* (Rome: Pontifical Biblical Institute, 1969).

Rawlinson, A., *St Mark* (London: Methuen, 1925).

Reisner, Rainer, *Jesus als Lehrer: Eine Untersuchung zum Ursprung der Evangelien-Uberlieferung* (Tübingen: J.C.B. Mohr [Paul Siebeck], 3rd edn, 1988).

Rhoads, D., and D. Michie, *Mark as Story: An Introduction to the Narrative of a Gospel* (Philadelphia: Fortress Press, 1982).

Riesenfeld, H., 'Tradition und Redaktion im Markusevangelium', in W. Eltester (ed.), *Neutestamentliche Studien für Rudolf Bultmann zu seinem siebzigsten Geburtstag* (Berlin: Alfred Töpelmann, 1954), pp. 157-64.

Robbins, V.K., *Jesus the Teacher: A Socio-Rhetorical Interpretation of Mark* (Philadelphia: Fortress Press, 1984).

Robinson, J.M., *The Problem of History in Mark and Other Marcan Studies* (Philadelphia: Fortress Press, 1982).

Roloff, J., *Das Kerygma und der irdische Jesus* (Göttingen: Vandenhoeck & Ruprecht, 1970).

Saussure, F. de, *Course in General Linguistics* (ed. C. Bally and A. Sechehaye in collaboration with A. Reidlinger; trans. W. Baskin; New York: Philosophical Library, 1959).

Schenke, L., *Studien zur Passionsgeschichte des Markus: Tradition und Redaktion in Markus 14.1-42* (Stuttgart: Calwer Verlag, 1967).

—*Die Wundererzahlungen des Markusevangelium* (SBB; Stuttgart: Katholisches Bibelwerk, 1974).

Schmidt, K.L., *Der Rahman der Geschichte Jesu: Literarkritische Untersuchungen zur ältesten Jesusüberlieferung* (Berlin: Trowitzsch & Sohn, 1919).

Schmithals, W., *Das Evangelium nach Markus* (OTNT; Gütersloh: Gerd Mohn, 1979).

Schnackenburg, R., *The Gospel according to St Mark* (trans. W. Kruppe; New York: Crossroad, 1981).

Schreiber, 'Die Christologie des Markusevangeliums', *ZTK* 58 (1961), pp. 154-83.
Schweizer, E., *The Good News according to Mark* (trans. D. Madvig; Atlanta: John Knox Press, 1970).
—'Neuere Markus-Forschung in USA', *EvT* 33 (1973), pp. 533-37.
—'Die theologische Leistung des Markus', *EvT* 24 (1964), pp. 337-55.
Stacy, W., 'Fear in the Gospel of Mark', (unpublished PhD dissertation, Southern Baptist Theological Seminary, 1979).
Steinberg, M., *Expositional Modes and Temporal Ordering in Fiction* (Baltimore: The Johns Hopkins University Press, 1978).
Suhl, Alfred, *Die Funktion der alttestamentlichen Zitate und Anspielungen im Markusevangelium* (Gütersloh: Gerd Mohn, 1965).
Sundwall, J., *Die Zusammensetzung des Markusevangeliums* (Åbo: Åbo Akademi, 1934).
Tagawa, K., *Miracles et evangile: La pensée de l'evangeliste Marc* (Paris: Presses Universitaires de France, 1966).
Tannehill, R., 'The Disciples in Mark: The Function of a Narrative Role', *JR* 57 (1977), pp. 398-400.
Taylor, V., *The Gospel according to St Mark* (New York: St Martin's Press, 2nd edn, 1966).
Telford, W., *The Barren Temple and the Withered Tree* (JSNTSup, 1: Sheffield: JSOT Press, 1980).
—*The Theology of the Gospel of Mark* (New Testament Theology; Cambridge: Cambridge University Press, 1999).
Theissen, G., *The Miracles Stories of the Early Christian Tradition* (trans. F. McDonagh; Philadelphia: Fortress Press, 1983 [1974]).
Tolbert, Mary Ann, *Sowing the Gospel: Mark's World in Literary-Historical Perspective* (Minneapolis: Fortress Press, 1989).
Trocme, E., *The Formation of the Gospel according to Mark* (trans. P. Gaughan; Philadelphia: Westminster Press, 1963).
Weeden, T.J., *Mark: Traditions in Conflict* (Philadelphia: Fortress Press, 1971).
Weiss, J., *Das älteste Evangelium* (Göttingen: Vandenhoeck & Ruprecht, 1903).
Wendling, E., *Die Entstehung des Markusevangeliums* (Tübingen: J.C.B. Mohr [Paul Siebeck], 1908).
Wohlenberg, G., *Das Evangelium des Markus* (Kommentar zum Neuen Testament; Leipzig: Deichert, 1910).
Wrede, W., *The Messianic Secret* (trans. J.C.G. Greig; Cambridge: James Clark, 1971 [1901]).
Wright, G.A., 'Markan Intercalations: A Study in the Plot of a Gospel' (unpublished PhD dissertation, Southern Baptist Theological Seminary, 1985).
Zerwick, M., *Untersuchung zum Markus-Stil* (Rome: Pontifical Biblical Institute, 1937).

Index of References